Groove Back
Lessons from a Life Coach
on Healing, Loving & Being Loved
After a Break-up or Divorce
by Kevin Anthony Johnson

Copyright 2018 Kevin Anthony Johnson

Names and details of specific persons and events have been changed to protect confidentiality. Plus, that just wouldn't be cool. The ideas and strategies proposed in this book are not to be taken as a substitute for professional mental health care or therapeutic counsel. There's nothing on how to get rich quick in here either. So….sorry. You are responsible for your own life and success. We're here to support, not enable you, so take responsibility for your own life. Is that alright?

All rights reserved. This book or any portion thereof may not be reproduced or used in any manner whatsoever without the express written permission of the publisher except for the use of brief quotations in a book review.

Editors:
Christina Motley
Trellis Usher-Mays
Julie Davidson-Gomez

To my three mothers:

Barbara Ann Lambert,
who so loved me she gave me to another.

My unknown caregiver for two years,
who gave me a happy space to grow.

Mary Dumas Johnson,
who made me her son and molded me into a man.

Introduction
Part 1: On Healing
Part 2: On Loving
Part 3: On Being Loved
About The Author

Introduction

CHAPTER ONE
Be Open to Possibilities

"Romance is about the possibility of the thing…When people who been together a long time say that the romance is gone, what they're really saying is they've exhausted the possibility."
—Darius Lovehall, Love Jones

Let's be real…relationships can be chaotic, messy, beautiful, destructive, nourishing, empowering and enlightening.

Forming them out of thin air can be terrifying to some and relatively easy for others.

In traditional dating, you and your date are attempting to meet, connect on some meaningful level, validate that connection and forecast the possibilities of a collaborative partnership - all within a single set of encounters over a very short period of time.

You bring all of your cultural history, family background, every past relationship, healthy or unhealthy, plus your own defense systems to avoid hurt or rejection into these encounters, and you hope that your date will see you accurately; "get" you; accept you "flaws and all," and maybe…just maybe, like you enough to invest more time getting to know you.

That's just the baggage from the past. Factor in the laundry list of expectations we intend to load upon our prospective partner and the weight becomes unbearable. We want it all: a soulmate, workout partner, best friend, parenting skills, financial, emotional and sexual prowess—not to mention the attraction factor. What we've come to call our "type" is probably the rarest human being alive.

With all of those ideals impacting our dating experience, I began to wonder how I could deconstruct modern dating. How could I more intentionally create the relationships that I wanted, versus my default experiences? At what point do my relationships (romantic or platonic) shift into my unconscious relationship story? What does it mean to date with clarity; to create experiences that foster mutual intimacy and awareness?

I saw that many of my relationships were following a pattern: I go out with somebody, have a good date, go out on another date and then I say, "Oh, well this is kinda getting interesting..so let me see where this goes..."

Instead of keeping a wider, more inclusive approach I went

down these narrow paths leading me into a long term relationship. At the very beginning, I let certain things slide because I was operating from my own scarcity thinking. I lacked a sense of abundance and felt there were limited options available to me, and that certain qualities I'd just have to learn to tolerate. Down the road those same qualities I allowed to "slide," became the very qualities that I couldn't stand. After a number of cycles I realized that I chose each of these situations, that's who that person is. It's not their fault. The responsibility was 100% mine.

I literally set up my relationships for failure because I denied what I saw up front, and I didn't give myself the option of seeing the other possibilities before making a decision to enter a relationship. I also didn't develop the sensitivity to be able to discern what was sustainable for me and my well-being.

So my advice to you at the start, is to hold your mind open to the possibility that your approach to dating has been flawed—perhaps at its core, the idea of dating is flawed. To think that in a few encounters we can somehow determine the viability of relationship success is comical. Yet, this is the myth we've been taught by songwriters and Hollywood producers—that love is magical and mysterious. We've been taught this, and maybe we've become promoters of it in the memes and table conversations we have about relationships. Just search #relationships on any social media platform and stare in awe of the flood of relationship advice—often nonsensical and mostly contradictory. My work in this book is to support you in questioning the way you've always approached relationships.

Questions for Reflection:

1) Are you open to the possibility that there's a more nourishing relationship waiting for you to help create it?
2) Are you open to unlearning the old dating ways and experimenting with new ways of knowing yourself and sharing your authenticity with another human being?
3) How open can you become?

CHAPTER TWO
The Challenge of Dating

The concept of dating has countless definitions today. From a casual fun outing to casual sex to serious relationship prospecting, it seems that there is no shared definition that guides today's experience of dating. Heck, my life partner just recently told a new friend that we've been "dating" for 2 years. (???) We got a good laugh about that, but this lack of shared understanding has become a huge problem. Two people with two very different definitions and expectations will be very frustrated without a shared view on what dating means to them.

How do we discuss the nature of our relationship? How do we know we're speaking the same language?

For the purposes of this book, I define a date as a space or time set aside for an encounter between two people, interested in the possibilities and synergies of relationship. The purpose of a date is to test relational possibilities. This applies to teenagers, college students, young adults, single adults, LGBTQ and married couples. It's about excavating possibilities. When we stop noticing what is right in front of us, out of familiarity, overwhelm or indifference, we begin to lose sight of what's possible. We resort to primal strategies to get our needs met, while the human spirit yearns for a higher level of expression and engagement.

With the mass adoption of dating apps and off/online matchmaking services, I sensed a renewed need for strategies to navigate this evolving relationship landscape.

To clarify, no one actually "dates" online. Apps and sites are designed to help us filter and screen our dating prospects. I know of many hopeful men and women who say they are frustrated with these new tools, because they don't like to spend weeks chatting with random people who have shown interest in them. We cannot test relational possibilities through an online profile and a casual swipe. We cannot test these possibilities with chat or text. Still, so many will complain about their disappointment with the technology of dating when they've never even started the dating process.

The point of these apps and sites is to move you from one level of connection to another. If you like someone's profile, and they like yours, you match and have time to chat or call each other to determine whether you want to move to a higher quality interaction – perhaps face to face. If you're not interested, you are empowered to end the connection and move along.

But what does it mean to have "movement" in these early stages of dating?

All relationships move—some slower or faster than others. We know a relationship is moving positively when the intimacy is growing. A word, time, gesture, a feeling expressed, these all prompt a relationship to change position and reflect the quality of the intimacy. Movement is at the core of getting our groove back. Inversely, a relationship can move away from intimacy due to resistance or blockage in the flow of mutuality between a couple. Here is where we run into problems: we want the relationship to move, but each of us brings our own degree of resistance to intimacy into every date and subsequently, every relationship. Part of this comes from the mythology we have grown up expecting to experience: The rescuing prince; the damsel in distress; the pygmalion transformation into the ideal man or woman and Sleepless in Seattle/Love Jones/When Harry Met Sally kind of memes in our collective mind. We want to experience the Hollywood moments: the meet-cute, the thrill of a first kiss, the deep gaze and a hand at the small of the back. These are all wonderful moments, but they are not the right things to evaluate your match or a new relationship by.

No wonder we have very little clue on how to heal when those memes fail us. No wonder we wrestle with how to love someone with a different origin story—or be loved by them in return. Dating holds the hope of meeting the perfect match, while offering ourselves imperfectly. We know we've got work to do on ourselves, but we put our "best foot forward" until the match has earned our trust enough to show them who we really are—but the match has only grown to know our mask. That makes the unmasking a high-risk experience.

If we want our relationships to move, then we need to create the context for movement. The context is vulnerability. We experience what Kegan & Lahey have called "competing commitments" to revealing ourselves in a relationship. On one hand, we guard our hearts from rejection with our defenses and distance, while our other hand invites our date to get to know us. Our capacity to reveal ourselves is directly connected to our ability to develop deep, nourishing relationships.

As a father, I marvel at how easily babies play in the tub

together. There's no awkwardness, no shame, no judgements. They just joyfully play and splash and laugh. When do we lose that? At some point we are conditioned to believe that there's something bad about our nakedness. We judge the bodies of others and our own. We devise expensive ways to cover and enhance our nakedness with clothing and fragrance.

I've been a life and executive coach for over 20 years now, so I'm no stranger to the power of vulnerability. As I've worked with clients using the concepts of this book, I've observed that whenever transparency is modeled, it multiplies. When we move towards greater authenticity in a relationship, the level of mutuality and trust may exponentially grow as well. This calls for personal courage and a sense of adventure to explore the spaces beyond our comfort and isolation.

I documented my experience initially to document my awakening to the power of my own vulnerability in relationships—but not just in romantic relationships. These insights and a-ha moments extend to every single human connection in my life. If I want to create or deepen a human bond, then I go full-on vulnerable.

You may ask, "How is that different from a partnership? Or a friendship?" I agree. What is the difference?

If someone goes to the hardware store to buy a drill to hang oil paintings in her living room, what does she want? A drill? No. A hole in the wall? No. Art on her wall? Well, yes, but perhaps she ultimately wants to create a beautiful space in her home to retreat to and enjoy. The drill is simply a tool, not the final outcome.

The process is not the destination. Your intention for the

process determines your destination. It's possible for anyone to use the ideas that follow with an intention to manipulate or take advantage of others. If this is you, keep reading, you may change your mind by the end, and perhaps you'll understand why you hold such intentions at all.

What if your intentions are to pass the time? Just having fun? "Something to do?" I've heard a bunch of these intentions as I wrote this book and I only have one thing to say in response—if you're dating with those intentions, don't be shocked when you begin to date seriously and you encounter matches who are just passing the time, having fun, and now YOU are the something to do. If you're going to meet someone, have the intention of being authentic and curious about your match. Everything else is setting yourself up for chaos and confusion. If you don't bring an intention, someone may impose their intention on you.

As long as we're on this subject, let's just name the other intention often held in dating—fucking.

Let's not be prudish. This is a real mindset. Whether it's predatory or primal, the complexity this adds to dating has plagued and pleasured both men and women for thousands of years. It can be an intoxicating impulse, powered by our instincts for pro-creation and pleasure—not necessarily in that order. It is important to know what intentions are driving our dating experience, and equally vital to clearly share those intentions to whomever we are dating. Not doing so is flirting with drama, or more perilous outcomes. Own up to your dating intentions before asking another person out.

If your ultimate intention is to create the possibility of a beautiful space for a relationship, then this is a powerful model to get you there.

What if you could begin the dating experience in vulnerability? What if you put your whole self forward instead of your best foot? The risk for personal pain is potentially lower, as you're not as emotionally invested in the first encounter. The reward is a faster determination of how fit the match is for you based on their reaction to who you really are. You both find out quickly whether you are interested in learning more about the other.

That all sounds simple, but for those of us with any life experience, it challenges us to confront the demons of our past relationships, the fears, insecurities, hurts, rejections and letdowns of past relationships. This will call on us to excavate the mental models that got us to where we are, and build new ones that serve us far more effectively.

This is the essential direction of the book: helping you complete your past relationships, reinvent your mental models around relationships, and writing a new story of how you get your groove back in love and life.

CHAPTER THREE
How to Get the Most From This Book

There's no wrong way to consume this book. Return to the principles during your post-date reflection time and think about what that particular idea means for you in that moment. The meaning will evolve over time as you engage in your own dating experiments. It may be interesting to join other friends and share your learnings in order to cross-pollinate and encourage each other. Take in the assignments and give yourself time to process each experience well.

Since this is an alternative way of thinking about developing relationships, there should also be a new kind of language as well. To make this book more conversational, let's just call anyone you're connecting with a "match," regardless of how you met them. At some point, you swiped right on them, or at least you did so in your mind. So for the rest of our time here they will simply be called matches.

DISCLAIMER: To protect the identity of all matches mentioned here, I've replaced their names with a descriptive title that starts with B. I don't know exactly why I chose that letter—perhaps it was Beyonce-inspired— but it made perfect sense when I was writing the first draft, so I've kept it in the book.

Another term I'll use often is "data." Data is simply the information that you will be gathering and using to form your opinions about each dating encounter. You'll pick up valuable data the more you "tune in" to your match.

His first text is "Wassup?" That's data.
   She answers the phone, "Yeah?" That's data too.
   He waits for you at the door of the coffee shop and offers to pull your chair out to sit. That's data.
   She says, "I can do that myself, thank you." That's data too.
   He sets his phone on the table at the beginning of your date. Data.
   He answers his phone while you're talking to him. Da.ta.

I've come to look at everything as data. How you engage me in the pre-date; how you communicate by text; how you communicate by phone; how you communicate by Skype. Do you communicate at all? Do you respond within a day? A week?

Early on, I noticed that it was very easy to miss these nuggets of insight if I wasn't also paying attention to what I have come to call "hooks."

A hook is any action, quality or experience that takes you off balance and makes it near impossible to see even the most obvious data someone is giving you. How attractive someone looks; how safe someone seems; how rare a person seems to be; and how impressive someone's LinkedIn profile looks - these all can cause you to overlook the way your date is showing up right now. We'll go into greater depth later on.

The holy grail of this approach is your emerging Partner Vision (PV). As you apply the principles to your dating encounters and get to know yourself along the way, you'll also be slowly building an increasingly clear vision of the partner you yearn for. Each date becomes a jot of color used to craft your masterpiece. You never waste a date, because each outing reveals something to you that you like or dislike. Each experience reveals something about you, too—if you're paying attention.

There are literally thousands of resources on building online dating profiles, so I won't spend much time in the details of that stage of the process. I focus on what I did and what worked for me. I'll share my own preferences, but ultimately you will figure out what represents you in the most authentic fashion.

Let this book raise your awareness, challenge your long-held assumptions and help you stay emotionally fit for the adventure. Keep it on your phone. Listen to the audio. Refer to it often, bookmark it in your Kindle app. Highlight the sections that resonate with you.

Don't just read this and think "this is a really good idea!"

That's not the point either. Talk about these ideas with friends. Hand a copy to your teenager. It's not simply a "how to" book, but more of a handbook of principles and observations that are worth debating and testing in your own world. Let's get into it.

Part 1: On Healing

CHAPTER FOUR
How It All Went Down

I closed the door as she walked down the stairs of my 4th floor walkup on the South Side of Chicago. Wiping the tears from my eyes I couldn't help but feel awash with a mix of despair and relief that she was gone.

I was in a storm of remembrance of what it felt like to move away from my extended family and close cousins in Cincinnati, Ohio when the Ford Motor Company transferred my father to Detroit, Michigan to lead several projects when I was 8 years old; the trauma and disarray of being evicted at 18 from the home I'd grown up in and living out of garbage bags while staying with friends and in hotel rooms for almost 2 years; the anguish of losing my mother to lung disease when I was 28, while also being relieved that she wasn't suffering anymore. This was one of those lows—and the contrast between this low and the high I was coming down from was staggering.

In the last 10 years, I'd moved to Chicago and went from coaching total strangers at the 24-hour Starbucks in Chicago to coaching leaders around the world. I'd just spent the last 10 months coaching across 7 time zones, traveling to Shanghai, China and the Netherlands working with 47 senior leaders from the largest consulting firm in the world. I was their team coach, helping them navigate the intercultural and interpersonal challenges that came up as they worked on their global projects. Much of my career as a coach has been in support of self-awareness, leadership, communication and relationships – and I was at the top of my game. The only thing better than this was being a father to my three children.

I was riding a massive wave of goodness. The week I met her, I'd just been reunited with my birth family after forty-five years of separation, after a miraculous chain of events led me to my blood brother's front door in Toledo, Ohio. That following Friday, she & I went on our first date, and within three months we were engaged. Two months later, she and her young daughter moved in.

It all happened so fast. Too fast.

I was rushing my way into a relationship, riding that wave of good feelings and ignoring the emotions of fear and clues of dysfunction and disconnect. My body began to respond to the cluster f#$k of growing relationship tension, a master's degree thesis deadline and the impact of over 120,000 miles of travel in a single year – I was diagnosed with a severe sleep disorder, pre-diabetic symptoms and severe clinical depression.

I had no idea how to end the free fall. My doctor prescribed six weeks of medical leave for me to give space and time for healing that my body and mind badly needed.

It was total chaos.

I was hurting – and hurt people, hurt people. For the next three weeks of medical leave my fiancé and I waged verbal and emotional warfare upon each other until it was too much for either of us to bear. I'd grown close to her daughter and it tore me apart to think that I would inflict the same separation upon her that my own life had been infused with.

One morning she suggested that she move out, and I agreed, marking the beginning of the end of our relationship. I spent the next two months alone and reflecting on my life and trying to mend my heart.

I went on walks on Chicago's beautiful lakefront, caught up with close friends and ate nourishing food – while I asked myself "who am I becoming?" I saw a therapist who challenged me to map out my relationship patterns and own my role in the success and unraveling of each of them. I let my body rest and my heart heal. Each of these acts of self-care were filling in gaps in my soul. They fed me. They invigorated me.

I saw a therapist for a few months before and several months after the breakup. She was a powerful woman of color who didn't take any BS from me. She called me out on my casual blaming of my fiancé as an oversimplification of our relationship and challenged me to own my part in the dynamics that led to the breakup. What did I know going into the engagement? What had I refused to acknowledge about her and how we got along? In order to change my story about love in my life, I did the work to understand the story I'd been habitually telling myself.

This is exactly what the word "relate" means. Relate translates literally to "tell again." When we repeat the old stories of love, family and relationship as if they are fixed and inflexible experiences, we are predicting future experiences and closing ourselves to the possibility of a new story writing itself into the pages of our life.

How we relate to love, becomes our story. Rewrite our story and we become the author of every relationship in our life.

One day I was talking with my friend Joe. We'd been friends since our days at Michigan State University and had shared parallel lives as we married, fathered our children, navigated divorce and figured out how to be single again. He reminded me of the natural ebbs and flows of life and that maybe I just needed to put myself out into the water and wait for the next wave to ride. I appreciated the analogy but Joe was also aware that I don't surf and I can't swim to save my life. Everyone needs a Joe in their life. I knew I wanted a great experience of love – but I'd been regularly sabotaging my pursuit of such an experience by avoiding the harder questions about my own value. He pulled me into taking bigger risks and helped me see possibilities that I was missing out on. One day Joe asked me, "Have you even met enough women to really understand what you're looking for?"

That was the question that started everything.

My friend's words lit a fire in me to not only get back out into the dating field, but to also confront the self-defeating elements within me that I'd been negotiating with for so long. This called for a radical departure from my status quo. I knew I was going to put myself "out there." I knew I wanted to broaden my experience, confront my fears and remove the layers of masks and erroneous beliefs that had historically marked my interactions in romantic relationships. I was terrified—and that's what let me know I really, really needed to give myself this experience.

I set out to meet and get to know as many women as I could

over the coming summer. I had no idea what that would actually mean. I had no idea I'd end up having over 100 dates in the next 100 days and learn lifelong lessons and transform my own way of being in the process.

That how it all went down. The rest of the book is coming back up from relationship failure. I'm not offering certainty of success- just a few breadcrumbs that you can choose to pick up if they seem right for you. It's about you knowing and honoring your inner voice and taking action. It's about getting your groove back.

CHAPTER FIVE
What's Your Origin Story?

"Possibility can work on us only when we have come to terms with our story. Whatever we hold as our story, which is our version of the past, and from which we take our identity, becomes the limitation to living into a new possibility."
Peter Block, Community

It's tempting to go from problem to solution. That's how our society likes to handle things—bandages placed over compound fractures. We're not going to do that here. In this journey we're about addressing the root of our patterns, so that's where we'll dig in.

Each of us has gathered a trunk-full of assumptions and beliefs about relationships, love, communication and sexuality across the years of our life. Even before puberty, you'd already formed many of the fundamental mental models you'd later use in every relationship.

My mother gave me to adoption services the day I was born. Being adopted at the age of 2, I never knew anything but my adoptive family until I began to question the difference in appearance across the faces of my younger brother, cousins and extended family. By age 11, I was asking too many questions for my parents to maintain the facade—so they told me the truth and it answered some questions and raised a few more. I'd already felt like an outsider. This is an inevitable outcome when nearly every adult in the family knows something the child doesn't. Family secrets might be kept silent, but they are felt. What mental models may have formed in me as a result?

I grew up figuring out ways to make myself fit in, be seen through doing projects that required my father to help me, or acting out in school to get my mother to rescue me from the "mean" male teachers at my all-boy high school. I got expelled three times in three years during high school. I'd clearly formed a model of women as rescuers, who I could rely on to hear and see me, and men as persecutors who were not to be trusted easily and always had exploitative motives toward me.

In my early 20s I began a program of self-development that led me to deeper understanding of all of the choices I made as a child in order to get through those developmental years. So many of my relationships reflected these simple, powerful models across every domain of my life. From mostly working for strong, creative women to marrying someone who rescued me during an emotional avalanche. Then encountering father-figure after father figure in my professional and personal life, who would use me for some gift or talent I held, then hold me at arm's length and deny any deeper mentoring or supportive relationship.

I'm telling you. This stuff runs deep. Does it surprise you that our relationships are so complex?

The assumptions I was operating from kept validating themselves. The more I looked, the more I saw data that supported what I was already feeling. This is what's called the Feedback loop. When we are looking for proof to support our assumptions, we inevitably get caught in a cycle of repeated experiences.

Have you ever found yourself dating the same "type" of person…even after swearing you'd never do that again? It comes back to the underlying assumptions we're walking around with, unquestioned and unexamined.

It's time to challenge these assumptions. They may have served you at the time—do they serve you now? Perhaps your belief system is built on the beliefs and worldview of your parents or other authority figures in your life. Some of these may still be valid, but give yourself the gift of reflecting on these beliefs with a critical eye. Are you living your life out of an obligation to live out their vision for you? Are you limiting your Partner Vision to those approved by their worldview? Are you living out someone else's dream for your life?

Ancient scriptures teach that as a child, you thought and acted as a child, but when you became an adult, you put away childish things. Childhood was your formation—now, in adulthood, you hold the reins to your transformation. This is the work. We are always working out our childhood into our adulthood. Relationships are no exception.

Let's explore how you're relating. I believe that gender is a continuum—that our binary approach to categorizing gender has created judgments and criticisms of others based on how our family or culture addressed expressions of gender and sexuality. In this book, I'll do my best to avoid the limits of male/female labels and invite you to explore your experience across masculinity and femininity instead.

Be aware, I'm not trying to challenge your values, but if your underlying beliefs are what has informed your values, you may have a moment or two where you rethink those values and come up with a new version of them.

Take a deep look into your origin story. Find the assumptions from your childhood and examine them for how they serve you today. Here's your workout:

Assignment:

1) Inventory your judgments and feelings and how they empower or disempower you.
2) Notice your thoughts and attitudes about those you would like to date.
3) Identify the ways your bosses, coworkers, and friends of other gender identities are similar to your Mom and/or your Dad.
4) What are my 3 top beliefs about the feminine and masculine in my life?
5) Where do these beliefs come from? Do they make relationships easier or more difficult?

CHAPTER SIX

Your Emotional History

Emotions can be confusing, unpredictable and terrifying at times. The range of feelings we experience daily as humans is often overlooked—muted by the noise in our minds and the distractions all around us.

But those emotions are there, nonetheless.

If you've ever had a "heated argument," then you've do doubt felt that warming sensation in your chest during an argument, or a flushing of your face during a conversation, or a tightening of your throat or chest during a stressful moment. You've just experienced a few of the physical signs of emotional energy.

My intention here isn't to teach a full course on emotional intelligence, but much of the literature on the subject is directed at business environments and "managing" your emotions—but how do you manage something you may not even be aware of?

And when it comes to relationships, there is a subconscious tendency to look for someone who can manage our emotions for us. We latch on to anyone who seems to be able to deal with or tolerate our unmanaged emotions.

What do I mean by unmanaged emotions?

I'm talking about incomplete emotional history—otherwise known as baggage.

Emotions, interrupted. We're all carriers. We're all lightening rods carrying emotional charges, in search of anyone more grounded than us, to offload the ever-growing spill-off of our incompletions.

Your history of emotions IS your history. The facts and details of your life are important, of course, but the emotional meaning you've attached to those events are the fundamental drivers for your belief system—how you relate to yourself, others and the world. We've all gathered a bunch of incomplete emotions, and this drives us in unconscious and conscious ways throughout our lives.

Think about that.

If you experienced trauma in your early childhood, your little self made sense of it in the best way you could. Maybe there were unspoken rules about affection, anger, crying or appearance that you conformed to because that was the only way for you to be a part of the family. You may have disliked these rules, but expressing your dislike could mean abandonment by your parents. This is how we think about the world as children. We make sense of things in the best way we can.

Fast forward to your last date: you're using a slightly adjusted version of your 7 year old map of the world, to navigate at age 39. You're still following those rules, even though you've moved out of your parents home and you've got your own life now—

those rules still govern how you're relating to your matches. Still holding back affection. Still playing "strong" to avoid the possibility of rejection. Still withholding tears because "men don't cry." Still maintaining that physique—not because you want to be healthy, but because you don't believe anyone will love you if you don't stay ripped.

Do you see how emotional incompletion can get in the way of relating to another human?

We call it baggage because it softens the blow of the real pain that's underneath our thin skins. Baggage makes it seems like something manageable and sometimes a bit of an annoyance.

Baggage is actually poison that we cover up with a glossy brand name and wear like we're going somewhere important.

You see, the original pain that created that baggage was healthy, normal emotional expression wanting to be released. The moment we close off that expression and withhold the free flow of emotion through our being, it begins to convert to a toxin. Just like when we were little, our beautifully complex mind moves quickly to push the deep hurt into the distance so we can continue to operate in the real world—but the emotion still wants to get out. It remains in our being, unexpressed and looking for a path to freedom. Ironically, we then build up defenses—a red line— against anyone touching those pain points, which also throttles down any expression of that pain.

Whenever someone begins to cross that red line, our defenses kick in and that person may see a side of us that they've never seen before. It might be shocking. It might be a dealbreaker.

Is there any wonder about why it's so challenging to date? THIS is what's going on behind the curtain of the person we present to potential matches. We're simultaneously searching for love, and searching for threats to our red line— at the same. Damn. Time.

You may want to rush into fixing this part of yourself right now. We'll get into a pathway to releasing and completing these emotions in a future pages. For now, sit with the emotions that are coming up for you right now. Grab a pen or your device and write what you're experiencing. Document any memories that rise up. Doodle and draw out the images surfacing in your mind. Allow those emotions to flow. Awareness is where this entire process begins. Resist the urge to fix, squash, cover, rationalize or minimize your feelings. Feeling is freedom.

Assignment:

1) What relationship pains are still circulating in your life?
2) What relationship situations to you notice you consistently avoid?
3) Who are you becoming, as a result of this assignment?

CHAPTER SEVEN

Your Relationship with Drama

One of the most impactful models I share with both business and personal clients is Stephen Karpman's Drama Triangle. Karpman captures one of the fundamental games we play with each other in relationship—avoiding responsibility.

How is this relevant to getting your groove back? It's EVERYTHING.

A relationship is built upon a mutual responsibility to myself and to my partner. The degree of personal responsibility both participants bring to the relationship can be a driving determinant of the success of that relationship. According to Karpman's model, drama involves the avoidance of responsibility by blaming others, enabling negative behavior or justifying one's own behavior.

To be clear, there is a difference between victimization and victimhood. There are REAL victims in the world. That's not what this model is about. Victimhood is an identity that we choose when we deny our personal power or agency in a given situation.

We're all guilty of playing least one of the key roles: victim, persecutor or rescuer. Let's explore how this factors in our dating and relationship experience—especially if you've had any relationship come to an end.

Drama thrives on our dwelling on our history or the future—the two realms that we have absolutely zero control over. We revisit our regrets and choices (good and bad) and then we worry over the consequences of actions we've yet to take.

The persecutor is intent upon blaming anyone other than themselves for the situation they're in. They're the finger pointers, the shamers, often so afraid of looking like a victim, they posture themselves as being powerful as they throw others under the bus. The victim is intent upon letting everyone know how life has "happened" to them. There's nothing they could've done. There's nothing they can do. Every possible solution is inadequate—because solving the problem would require them to actually take responsibility for their life in the moment. The rescuer is intent on making everyone feel better—and feel needed. Rescuers defend the victim, effectively keeping the victim safe in their victimhood, and justifies the persecutors by maintaining the status quo for everyone, while helping to change absolutely nothing.

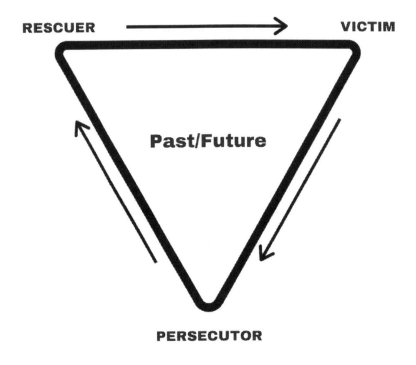

SOURCE: Stephen Karpman's Drama Triangle

As we venture back into dating and new relationships, some of the biggest hurdles to overcome are the triggers of our accumulated relationship experience. If we felt like victims in our last relationship, you may withhold your real opinion or be hypersensitive to persecutor behavior and overreact to assertive actions. If you were historically more like the rescuer, you may feel an urge to defend or save your date, when the data you're gathering from them is telling you to move on. If you're historically the persecutor, you may not be aware of how you're affecting those you're interested in and be confused as to why you're not getting second dates or callbacks.

These behaviors aren't accurately representing you. But they become the only experience your date has of you—so it's vital that we become aware of these habits. How are you showing up? Victim? Rescuer? Persecutor?

Drama limits our vulnerability. We get out of this vicious cycle by taking full responsibility for our experience in the moment. Get out of the past and the future and step into the here and now.

When we are focused on the present moment it's far harder to slip into drama-thinking.

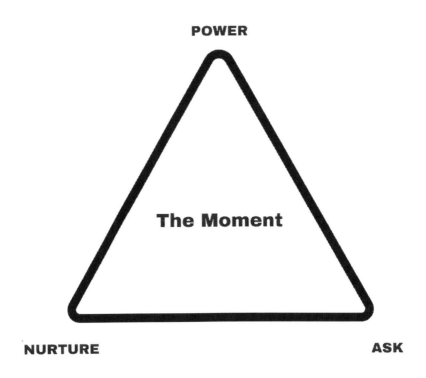

Adapted from Stephen Karpman's Drama Triangle

In the moment, we have better choices to choose from. Instead of playing the victim, we have a choice to ask for what we need from those around us, and still hold full responsibility for our satisfaction in life.

Instead of persecuting, we can challenge and provide support and boundaries. Instead of being victim we can use our voice and ask for what we need from those around us and take informed action. Instead of rescuing, we can respond to the needs of others, and empower them to take ownership of their lives.

Doesn't that sound like the perfect relationship? Isn't supporting, challenging, speaking up, responding to each others needs, empowering and taking action what we desire in our relationships?

In your future dates, give attention to how much drama shows up during your conversations. How much is your date empowering you, asking for what they need and providing nourishing support? How "in the moment' are they? How about you?

Full responsibility looks like interdependence, accountability and empowerment. Let this be a simple measuring stick for those you meet—and for your own presence as you step into this journey.

ASSIGNMENT:

1) What's your relationship with drama?
2) How have these roles shown up in your past experiences?
3) What triggers may be driving your encounters as you date new matches?

CHAPTER EIGHT

The Emotional Fitness Model

> "Our job is unconditional love.
> The job of everyone else in our life is to push our buttons."
> —Byron Katie

A key element of my dating journey was honoring my emotional journey as well. With every encounter I was increasingly engaged and practicing authenticity and vulnerability. This came with a cost. Sometimes I experienced a high, and other times I left a date in a low place emotionally. I needed to be able to recover well from these experiences, and somehow come out stronger.

If you wanted to become stronger physically, you would begin a program of resistance training at a gym or at home. You might start with light weights and add weight each week as your strength and flexibility improved over time.

It's the same way with our emotional life. I call it emotional fitness.

You see, if physical fitness is measured by our speed to recovery (how quickly we can get back to our resting heart rate after physical exertion) then I suggest that emotional fitness is measured by how quickly we can repair the emotional "muscle tears" of the full range of human encounter.

Using this approach, you can slowly build your emotional fitness by fully engaging, then having some time to reflect alone or with a trusted friend on what emotions you're feeling and what you're doing with the information your emotions give you.

There are three stages in my model of emotional fitness, drawn from my experiences and a broad body of research around emotional and social intelligence. Let's walk through the model with one of my more..colorful..dates as an example:

Toward the midpoint of my 100 days, I connected with somebody to have a quick coffee date. The cafe was closing soon, so we decided to go to a bar nearby. We had a fun exchange and there was a playful chemistry, until she went off on a rant about her last boyfriend. "Kevin, he started coming home every night with pussy on his breath." Tears began to well up in her eyes and her mascara started to run while she took nervous, shaky sips of her red wine and recounted each of her ex's indiscretions. I began to scan the room rapidly for the server, thinking, "Check please…"

I sat across the table somewhat stunned at what I was witnessing. I felt both empathy and concern – and a good bit of fear. She was crying, but beneath those tears a deep anger was seething. It was as if I wasn't even there with her anymore.

Then, it happened.

She abruptly stopped her stream of consciousness heart dump, sat up straight, composed herself, grabbed her purse and walked away from the table. At first, I thought she was going to clean up the mascara that had run rampant down her cheeks, but she passed the restrooms and went right out the front door!

No goodbye. No eye contact. Nothing.

I paid for our drinks and went home bewildered. The next morning she sent a text asking, "WTF happened last night Kevin?" and after typing and deleting at least three different scathing responses, I decided to type back, "You did. Goodbye," (and a subsequent mobile number block.)

That was a massive download of data there. Aside from my suspicion that she blacked out during our date, she didn't come across as even remotely READY for a date, let alone a relationship. She needed to heal from a ton of hurt she was still overwhelmed with.

As a seasoned life coach, I realize that I often create spaces where people feel safe enough to disclose at very deep levels. I cannot ride a bus or train without someone telling me their life story, but that night I showed up for a date, not a coaching session.

You're going to run into people whose level of emotional fitness reveals itself, perhaps in the form of oversharing, as the example above reflects. You will also see this in the form of immaturity, how they interact with servers, how they tip or even something as simple as being able to decide what to order. It's all data.

Here are the three phases of the Emotional Fitness Cycle with this date in mind:

Feeling is our experience of the core emotions of fear, hurt, anger, sadness and joy. There are many other emotions but this is a simple list to draw from. The work of feeling is to first acknowledge they are actually surging within us at all times. Unfortunately our Western culture has given us more tools to mask our feelings than to express them. Emotional fitness gives us a "gym" to unmask these emotions and experience them in the moment.

Begin by searching your physical person for signs of tension, rushes of heat and visible signs of flushing in your face and neck. Then reflect on what triggered those effects. What were the words, actions, perceptions that informed your reaction? The purpose of this phase is to take in as much emotional information as you can, then move on to the Dealing phase. Here's my process:

> I had a good time for most of the evening. I felt some joy in the interaction. She was funny. When she began her rant, I felt as if she was abandoning me, which stirred up some old pain around my adoption and several previous relationships, and then she really DID leave me and left the bar. This left me both speechless and hurt. Her text the next day triggered both hurt and anger at her total obliviousness to how she affected me.

Dealing is our process of making sense of our feelings. How we make meaning of our experiences is how we build our lives. Each experience allows us to make some meaning of it, and we can take a drama role or a responsible role in the meaning we make of our lives. This is done in times of reflection, as we make connections between our feelings and our historical experiences. Was my reaction based on this present moment, or some past event that came to mind? Was my date's emotional implosion the result of something I did to her, or was she caught in a cycle of trauma from her past? Take the time to discuss your feelings, reactions and emerging patterns with a friend, loved one or even a therapist. Here's how I reflected on it:

> Her actions weren't about me at all. She was in a great deal of pain and I'd naturally provided a safe place for her to "dump" that pain. In the moment I felt hurt and angry, but as I realized that her actions weren't really directed at me, I felt compassion for her. I recalled my time of healing after my marriage fell apart. I felt shame, as my initial response was to dismiss her and block her from my phone out of my own hurt.

Healing is the final stage in the Emotional Fitness Cycle. How do you help yourself recover from relationship wounds? Perhaps in the past you've resorted to binge eating, dating diets, binge sex or other extreme measures that only mask the hurt you've experienced. To really heal, you can turn to nourishing experiences. Find ways to nurture yourself, rebuild your self-love and feed your soul with reading, art, music and community. Contrary to popular memes, I don't believe that time heals our emotional wounds. Time is simply a container for our choices. If you fall into the trap of "how things should be" you may be unknowingly prolonging the pain and time to recovery. Let go of your "should" and embrace this moment, then choose how you want to feel right now. When you decide to be healed, you will be begin healing. As you focus on surrounding yourself with wholeness, you will be surprised to discover that you, too, are whole, and ready to re-engage.

> You might be asking, "What does HE have to heal from?" Here's where we often miss the growth opportunities from dating. Every encounter costs us something emotionally. We become vulnerable, show ourselves authentically, listen deeply and practice curiosity. Healing is what happens when we give to ourselves what we (hopefully) gave our date – honesty, attention, care and inquiry. Treat yourself to time alone, exercise, meditation, journaling, live music, sit in front of a body of water or in spiritual fellowship. Feed your body, mind and spirit in the best way you can.

It's important to remember that as you are looking for someone special, you're also becoming 'that someone' for someone else. Take the time to recover after every encounter. Pray, meditate, smudge yourself with some smoldering sage – do whatever it takes to process and clear your heart after such a good workout.

Look for someone who can meet you at your level of emotional fitness; someone who could stretch you; who can be emotional workout partners with you. Partners should bring equal value to the table. This is a lifetime journey of building your emotional Self one encounter at a time.

ASSIGNMENT:
1) How emotionally fit are you today?
2) Where do you notice emotional sensitivity?
3) What "gets" to you early in a relationship?
4) How long does it normally take for you to recover from an emotional hurt?

CHAPTER NINE
You & Your Partner Vision

This is a deep dive into who you are and what you want in a relationship. I've observed over my years of ministry and coaching people from all walks of life, that we are very quick to demand certain qualities from our desired partner. We expect them to be everything.

This is a ruse.

Many of the best relationships I've observed have origins like this:

"I didn't really find him attractive when we met."
   "We really felt like oil and water on our first date."
   "I was angry with my friend for setting us up. We had NOTHING in common."

There's a trend here.

We all have egos that tell us that the best person for us should be similar to us, have similar interests, similar passions and dreams. Then, after some time around that "perfect" person, those very traits that attracted us begin to annoy the f@$% out of us. This is, of course, a choice that we all can make. There's nothing wrong with this path. And yet, I want to suggest a different way.

Explore deep differences as you date. Be curious and see where a match might stretch your boundaries a bit. Carol Dweck, author of the best-seller Mindset: The New Psychology of Success, describes what she calls a Growth Mindset, which is a belief that one can develop new skills over the course of one's life. Her findings support my own belief that relationship skills are the same way. By breaking the pattern of choosing the same "type" of person you've always dated, use the practice of EveryDay Dating to experiment with matches who you'd probably never have matched with by your old criteria. Open your filter up and try this next move on for size:

Filter with your values.

Yes, remove the superficial, material filters and connect with what's most important to you. I'm not saying you should go out with someone you can't stand to look at, but I think it's fair to say that most of us have been conditioned to think we must have some manner of "ideal" partner. This, again, is from our childhood conditioning.

I challenge you to look at your own actions and choices over the past 2 years and explore what values you have been practicing—not talking about—PRACTICING. Our choices are our values in action. Perhaps, as you evaluate your actions, you may see a pattern that you don't really align with. In this case, you have discovered an incongruence between your actions and your stated values.

This is what makes dating a difficult activity to navigate. We may say we hold certain values as we seek a partner in life, but in practice we are holding very different values. Before you swipe right on anyone else, take some time to figure out what you ACTUALLY value in a relationship. This will inform your Partner Vision.

Your Partner Vision should reflect the values that you hold essential for your nourishment within a relationship. I value belonging, excellence (not perfection) and growth. As I went on my 100+ dates, it became very clear to me who aligned with these values and who didn't. This isn't about another laundry list. This is your clarity around how you want to experience partnership. This is not judgmental either. It is a matter of alignment. Those who didn't align with me will no doubt align with someone else whose values are similar. By filtering by values, you also create a useful guard against the hooks covered in the chapters ahead.

There's another benefit to filtering matches by your values: everyone lives out their values differently. This means that you may value creativity and express it in your painting, while someone else may value creativity too—and express it in creating new business models for entrepreneurs. Same value, different expression. So the value frees us from the tyranny of sameness that plagues so many single people. We seemingly can't help but find more of ourselves, unless we take intentional action to curate a different dating experience for ourselves.

My Partner Vision read as follows:

> She values both togetherness and solitude; serious play and intense work; teaching and learning. She is willing to see me as flawed as I am, yet still embrace me in my imperfection, yet still challenge me to be more of Who I am. She nourishes my mind, heart and body.

Do you see how this Partner Vision can inform my dating experience? From this rubric, I can use my time spent with each match, evaluating how each one fits within this vision. I can ask questions that explore how they express these values? Do you enjoy spending time alone? What was your last day off spent doing? Tell me about your circle of friends. What topics are you curious about? What matters most to you? This is the level of questioning that break through the BS of modern dating.

Try this for yourself, here's your homework:

ASSIGNMENT:
1) Make a list of your top 10 values
2) For each value, reflect over the past year on how you've acted out these values
3) Prioritize your values.
4) Select the top three values form your list. Write what each value means to you and what that value looks like in action.
5) Write your own version of the Partner Vision

CHAPTER TEN

The Practice of Everyday Dating

You've worked through your origin story, your relationship history and a model for Emotional Fitness, now let's get into even more juicy stuff. If you're coming out of a healing time in your life and just venturing back into the dating space, this is where things get recharged and you begin to put the previous work into practice.

During any recovery, there's a period of time called rehabilitation—this is where we restore the functional ability to connect, give and receive emotional nourishment from others romantically. Everyday Dating is my approach to rehab. Now, you may see why we needed to walk through the emotional fitness model BEFORE getting into the new dating mindset. You're going to be using different relational muscles now—and perhaps using a few muscles that you've allowed to atrophy and become less effective. All of the effort you historically put into looking amazing on the outside is now going to be evenly split between the inner and outer presentation of yourself. We're working on your core now. This might make you feel a

CHAPTER ELEVEN
The Five Wicked Hooks

We're about to get into the "nitty gritty" of getting your groove back. This is where you begin to get back "out there" and meet new people and learn more about yourself than you may ever have. Before we dive into the dating approach, I want to make sure we prepare for the inevitable traps along the way.

As you engage with your dates, it's important to pay attention to a few important sensations. These sensations are what I call "Hooks." Hooks cause us to overlook otherwise obvious words, behavior and other cues that our date is giving us. You may experience a hook as feeling unable to resist a quality in someone despite your awareness of other qualities that you don't enjoy or resonate with. These hooks represent challenges to your values, integrity, character and self-esteem.

Perhaps more precisely, hooks pull you away from your authentic self. They place distance between who you really are and what you really yearn for. Hooks pull us out of our spiritual center and disconnect us from our internal guidance system of intuition, values and higher aspirations, drawing us approval, safety, survival. They dilute our decision-making power and cause us to hand over that power to those primal influences.

When you experience a hook, you may notice a strong desire to negotiate with yourself. You may want to defend your reasoning and talk yourself out of listening to the information right in front of you. Here, I'll describe four hooks that I've identified. I'm sure there are many others, but I've managed to consolidate my experiences into four types of hooks:

CHAPTER TWELVE
Attraction

The first hook is attraction.

What I've come to realize is that beauty (or what our Western concept of beauty looks like) affects us as we grow up. We're conditioned to want to be beautiful and to be around so-called beautiful people. So of course, when we begin to think about relationships, how someone looks can be a powerful driver in our experience.

There's nothing wrong with being attracted to someone. To the contrary, attraction is often the catalyst for contact. It's when that attraction overrides other relevant information from our heart and mind, that we can set ourselves up for deep disappointment.

I matched with a smart-looking and gorgeous media professional. Notice my evaluation of her intelligence, based off of virtually nothing but her profile on Tinder. My profile contained the language stating "I'm ready" for a relationship. In her first message to me, she wrote: "Wow, I don't know how ready I am, I'm kind of a commitment-phobe." (We'll come back to her words later.) We continued to chat and planned to meet within the week. I overrode my entire micro-date strategy and planned a full dinner date. I was already hooked.

On date night, I practiced all of my breaths and we had nearly 5 hours of time together. We held hands, walked through neighborhoods, and had plenty of good eye contact throughout the evening. We kissed as I dropped her off to her place - another break from my dating approach - and I drove away thinking this was the best date yet!

Two days later, I hadn't heard from her. No response to my call or text. Finally she sent a long text explaining that she wasn't interested.

I was devastated. More importantly, I'd been hooked like a deep sea tuna fish. This was more than a blow to my ego. This felt like abandonment—one of my major developmental issues as an adoptee. I'd bared much of my soul with her in a short period of time and had it handed back to me crumpled like a discarded page of a book. This is always the risk of getting naked. I needed to dig into my experience and get the lessons from it.

I'd ignored the early data that SHE provided. She literally told me she wasn't sure of her own readiness for something serious, and that she shunned commitment.

Emotional Fitness: As I reflected on this experience, I realized that I'd done this exact same thing a few years earlier to a onetime date. This was my own "chicken coming home to roost." I ghosted on someone who I was afraid to engage with because I sensed it was going somewhere I didn't want it to go. I was too "chicken" to say so, and I hid. This stuff ain't always pretty and glamorous. Sometimes your fears will get the best of you, as they did me. It's ok. Get back up and into the field again.

It took me a couple of days to get my dating rhythm back (check out the chapter on emotional fitness to see how I did this on a regular basis), but it was a powerful lesson and a turning point for me. Attraction is good, but it is only a portion of the information someone gives you. Take all of the data into consideration as you figure out who you want to stay engaged with. No matter how visually appealing, know that the exterior is a temporary feature, and for the kind of bond that endures, we need to be mindful of the whole person.

That being said, it is also possible to be hooked in reverse on this one. Our social constructs about beauty, facial appeal, weight, and even ethnicity, can all hinder our experience and possibly limit our options – but what do any of those things have to do with finding authentic love? In my experience, I swiped right on women who didn't match my usual preferences because I wanted to make sure I wasn't cutting myself off from the kind of person I was compiling in my heart and mind during this process. I went out with different body types, heights, weights and ethnicities. I learned so much from each of them and I don't regret a minute of my time invested in getting to know so many different women.

Embrace the attraction, but don't allow it to hook you as you evaluate all of the other information your match is offering to you. Notice what is consistently attractive to you, and keep building a composite of your ideal partner as you learn and grow.

Unhook yourself from Attraction.

CHAPTER THIRTEEN
Impression

The second hook is the hook of impression

We've been conditioned to appreciate a good first impression. A warm smile, firm handshake, a contemporary, fashionable look – these might be the things that tell us, "This person seems like they're well put-together."

The key word is "seems."

Being is not the same as seeming. I'm not saying you shouldn't enjoy the sharp-dressed man or woman across from you, but keep a steady heart. Sometimes the skill of presentation is the totality of what a person has to offer, so they invest in it with abandon. If you get caught up in the presentation, you may not notice the absence of substance underneath the shiny veneer.

Perhaps they are intelligent, well-spoken, well-read and worldly, having traveled well. Maybe they show a high level of intellectual ability, spiritual or professional compatibility. These are all wonderful traits, and they can add tremendous richness to a relationship, but ask more questions. They can also be the mask your match wears to cover their weaker side.

I challenge you to ask more complex questions of someone who looks exceptional at first glance.

- Regarding your life decisions thus far, how would you evaluate them?
- What have you learned from past relationships?
- If you were to lose it all today, what would you rely on to help you rebuild?
- What's the second thing that people remember about you?

I've been duped on a few occasions by an amazing resume or a glowing LinkedIn profile—only to discover she was simply very skilled at word-smithing. I've spoken with matches whose dating profile oozed professionalism and class, but on our first micro-date, it became clear through her treatment of cafe staff and her public sharing of private talks with her friends, that we were not a good fit.

Character will bleed through shiny packaging eventually. The micro-date is your best chance at filtering for inauthenticity. It's also a chance to look within, and uncover the ways in which this hook drives you.

Unhook yourself from Impression. Catch yourself being impressed and get back to noticing what's really happening in the encounter.

CHAPTER FOURTEEN
Security

Another hook is security.

We are hooked by a sense of security when someone offers us something "familiar" about how they relate to us. Perhaps they remind us of what we enjoyed in our last relationship, or even qualities slightly better. But do you want your next relationship to be slightly better, or transformational?

The hook of security is a subtle tug back into your relationship pattern. You know this pattern well. Even if it is dysfunctional, it's what you've become comfortable with, so there's nothing challenging you to grow or leave bad habits behind.

Then there's the security of transaction. You give something, you get something. I think this is even more treacherous, because we can slip into this without being fully aware of our dependency that is developing, and how we might be overriding our intuition and all of the data the other person may be giving that would otherwise send us running in the other direction.

We transact our talents and skills in exchange for money - we all do that to some degree. However, when someone doesn't realize this kind of transaction is happening, that's when it's dangerous. That's when it becomes harmful. Unconscious pursuit of security can place us in relationships where we hand over our power to another - sugar daddies and sugar mommas come to mind. We may begin to make life choices based on maintaining the security this person provides, instead of developing and maintaining a security in and of ourselves.

Notice when you feel something familiar. It's tempting to interpret this as a "kindred spirit" sensation, like you've known someone before. Stay curious and question that sensation. What is this person stirring up within me that seems so familiar? Is this a re-packaging of my last relationship? Is there an element of position or power that is drawing me to them?

Again, the hook by itself is simply data for you to evaluate and make sense of. Your work is to see the hook for what it is - an excuse for you to rationalize contradicting information.

For me, there comes a time when the "tried and true" ceases to serve my dreams, when "safe" really means "stagnant" and "secure" really means "resistant" and I decide to create a new space for growth.

I realize this might seem scary to some, but I'm asking you anyway:

What new space do you need to create? What has been safe and familiar to you? Is it still serving you and the person you're becoming?

Unhook yourself from Security

CHAPTER FIFTEEN
Scarcity

The final hook I'll cover here is Scarcity.

Scarcity shows up in a multitude of ways. If you're on a date and you're thinking:

- This is the last date I may ever be on;
- I want this ONE to like me sooooo bad;
- I can't get any better than this;

—you might be hooked in scarcity.

This one's personal for me. As an adopted kid and child of divorce, I built an identity around scarcity. It infused my views on everything from my education and career to family and money. I simply struggled with holding an abundant lens on the world.

In dating, scarcity nudged me to accept whatever life presented me, instead of seeking what inspired me. Scarcity will have you grateful for mediocre experiences and might even ask you to lower those expectations.

The hook of scarcity grabs everyone at some point in their life. It may not be about money, but it certainly can be about a lack of love and connection in your life – the pain of loneliness. This pain drove me to partners who were in just as much pain as I was – and then we were in pain together, but neither was less lonely.

You feel it as you prepare for an interview.
   You sense it when you're looking for a parking space.
   You are reminded of it every time you have to wait in line.

There seems to be only so much love, help, companionship, time, money to go around.

Yet, this is only true if we are powerless and inactive agents in life. You are resourceful and you've already proven that by seeking out the contents of this book. You are capable of creating as much love, asking for the help, reaching for the companionship, making the time and creating the value that money will respond to. You can do all of these things.

The only scarcity that is real, is a scarcity of belief.

As you work through this hook, you'll notice moments where you awaken to the ocean of abundance around you, then slip back into scarcity thinking. This is normal, just notice it and get familiar with what brings this on in your life. In that moment, what are you being asked to accept? What standard are you lowering? What single action would raise your emotional expression?

Again, this hook asks you to stay small enough to fit the limiting space of your life, while you've outgrown that container and require expansion. Scarcity comes to tell you that you don't deserve that new space to grow; that if you take that space, someone else won't grow. Only so many people can have great love in their life, and perhaps you're not one of "them." All. Lies.

Notice when you're feeling small. Notice those hints at inferiority. Notice when you're about to resign and accept less than what you yearn for.

Unhook yourself from Scarcity.

CHAPTER SIXTEEN

Overcoming the Hooks

How do you overcome these hooks?

The answer is probably counterintuitive: bring them out into the open. The power of a hook is held in the very vulnerable place. When we "out" our own hooks they no longer can rule over our hearts and minds. Here's my suggested approach based on my own experience:

See the hook for what it is. As you notice the hook grabbing you, what is it telling you to do? The actions you feel compelled to take are the clearest clues to what you're being hooked by. Attraction asks for sex. Impression asks for the social approval of your network. Security asks you to declare your personal challenges. Scarcity compels you to settle and remain unsatisfied. When you catch yourself being tugged in any of these directions, pay attention, then…

Look for the hook in yourself. The hook is hooked in you. What has the hook found in you that it can grip onto so strongly? Attraction may hook onto my primal masculine drive to conquer a woman – disregarding her sacred femininity. Impression might push my ego to proudly parade and objectify a woman – minimizing her many other qualities. Security may cause me to shrink my own presence and elevate hers. Scarcity is desperation and the lowering of my values to retain the "connection" in front of me, as if she's the last woman on the planet interested in me.

Don't be fooled. Hooks will play some amazing tricks on you and you may not even notice them until you've already fallen for them. Be kind to yourself as you explore your hooks. I messed up often. You will too…it's okay.

Discuss the hooks that you're personally experiencing. Once you've identified the hooks affecting you, look for an opportunity to conquer them once and for all. I was talking with a very self-aware match, and though she didn't use these words, she basically caught me being hooked by impression. Her words were, "I hope you get that out of your system quickly." And within a few minutes we were beyond impression. As soon as you can, bring up you hooks in your dating discussions.

Try this: "I find you very attractive, but I want to set that aside for a while and get to know you beyond your looks. There are lots of attractive people, but I want to know the real you." Feel free to customize, of course, using your own values and vocabulary. When you begin to speak about these "secret" hooks, they magically begin to melt and lose their grip on you.

There are many other hooks that may present themselves. My aim here is to equip you with a few tools to manage them as they arise in whatever form they may. You can do this.

Assignment:
1) What hooks show up for you in your dating history?
2) What is the unmet need that might be helping that hook sink in?
3) How might you meet that need for yourself?
4) Who can you discuss these hooks with? Ask them to honestly give you feedback.

CHAPTER SEVENTEEN
Everyday Dating: Step by Step

EveryDay Dating is a simple model to follow.

That being said, it requires you to entirely let go of your previous way of thinking about dating. Your expectations are the chief enemy of a good experience.

If you go into it thinking, "I really just want to meet great people and learn something about myself," those are very loose outcomes. The outcome is achieved and you have reached your goal of meeting someone great and learning something about yourself. If you hold any other expectation, you may find yourself hooked and re-living old dating habits. Let. Them. Go.

Remember, this process isn't intended to find the mythical, magical "one" for you. It's designed to build your emotional fitness and equip you with the resilience and the tools to be ready to engage when great matches come along. The rest is up to you.

The purpose of the EveryDay Dating is to gather data. That's it.

You're gathering data about your match AND your reactions to them. Keep this at the forefront of your heart and mind as you practice this approach. The experience begins long before you meet your match face to face.

Let's take a look:

Step 1: Vanity Filter Removal

Take your usual filters off of your dating profile searches. Narrow your search to reflect your values around age and gender preferences, of course, but all of your standard vanity filters should go away. Eliminate scarcity by opening up to more possible matches. This is about learning, and you're not learning if you're going out on dates with the same types of people.

This means expanding your openness to other ethnicities too. Again, this is about questioning your assumptions, so play along with me okay? It's like international travel in your hometown and it can be an incredible journey if you dare to take the leap.

Step 2: Filter for Values

Your values help to govern and define who you are. Those values should be the only filters you put in place as you find matches and begin to engage by chat, text or phone. Let your values shine in your profile description. Let them ooze through your communications. Be yourself. Invite your match to do the same. Keep expectations simple and notice what your match is telling you along the way.

As much as you're showing your values, your match is seeing

them and evaluating for themselves whether you're a good fit for them too. You may leave the encounter with a friend or professional connection – or maybe the brief chat or phone call will be interesting enough to plan a face-to-face! You've done the values exercise, so pull that Partner Vision out and put it to use. You may tweak it along the way as you learn more about what you like and dislike.

Step 3: Connect & Collect

This is where you put your date detective hat on. Allow your curiosity to blend with your listening and give your date great questions to reflect and respond to. I personally like to begin with, "so, I know what you say about yourself on your profile (or other means of knowing them) but who are you, really?" Asking someone who they are is often the most difficult question to respond to. You're not trying to stump them.

The intent is to cut to the chase in a 20-30 minute conversation. With such a question, you give them an opportunity to remove their social mask(s) and offer them space to reveal themselves. I've often started a date by offering my own answer to that same question up front. I've found that by revealing myself first, it creates the invitation to be as open and authentic as I have been. Here are a few more tips on the date itself:

- Commit to genuine inquiry. Come to ask important questions and to learn from your match. Disengage from other communication sources and give your full attention to your match. Don't sit your phone on the table between you. Leave your phone off of the table. Put it in Airplane mode. Be present.
-
- Take risks, build trust and share. Reveal yourself with

every encounter. Share something you want them to know. Risk sharing a hook you've been caught by in the past.

-
- Let curiosity (and the data) lead you. Suspend your judgments. Be interested.
- Take special note of the body language of your date. What are they saying to you
- Notice their eye contact. What is it saying to you? Does the level of eye contact bother you?
- Now, pay attention to their words. Do they speak in monotone? Up speak? (that vocal tendency to end sentences as if they are questions?) (see what I did there?)
- Are you using your curiosity as you listen?
- What are they saying that "vibes" with you?
- What are the judgments that arise as you listen?
- Can you suspend those judgments and keep listening?
- What are they NOT saying?.
- Pay attention to the clues, verbal and non-verbal.
-
- Silence & Discomfort are OK. This is a great source of data. How someone deals with silence is closely related to their emotional fitness. Silence is where we go to feel, deal and heal. Notice how YOU handle silence: do you quickly move to fill it, or do you enjoy those gaps in conversation?

- Try your best not to go for closure. Unless you're certain you're not interested, keep the conversation open and following the stream of consciousness that shows up. If you're clear about your level of interest, BE CLEAR with your date. If you give mixed messages, expect a confused response.

Upon ending your encounter, you may decide how you want to proceed, or choose to wait until you can reflect more intentionally. If you want to see them again, say so, and set another time while you're in their presence. If not, shake their hand firmly and thank them for sharing a moment with you and leave.

Make sure your body language and your words match when you end the date. If you notice that these aren't in sync, check in with yourself about what you really want before ending the date. When in doubt, go out again and gather more data to make a better decision.

Step 4: Reflect & Refine

Now we build in your Emotional Fitness routine. Take the time to reflect on your experience with your match, make a note of things you enjoyed, or didn't. Pay close attention to how YOU felt during the exchange and what hooks may have surfaced.

- What grabbed you during the encounter? What was memorable? How does your match "fit" with you? What qualities did you appreciate? Which could you do without?

- How does your match add to your vision of a great partner?

- Determine how you want to move forward with this match. Will you have another encounter? Why? Perhaps more importantly, why not?

- How will you adjust your approach? Rethink what messages you're sending? Plan to reveal more about yourself next time?

- Be honest with yourself…are you hooked by something? Which hook & why do you think it affected you the way it did?

Emotional Fitness: Renew your commitment to yourself. Feel what you felt. Deal with the impact of this encounter. Heal yourself by reaching out for support and encouragement.

I was getting matches almost daily and sometimes it was overwhelming to deal with. I was getting behind on responding and I was resorting to copying, pasting and customizing my responses - not a good idea. One time I copied and forgot to customize and I called a really cute match the wrong name… needless to say I got quickly unmatched. Oh well. I learned to take my time and respond with short individualized messages with the intention of setting up either a call or a coffee date.

I began to take in every profile and every pre-date or pre-call experience as data for filtering through the noise of possibilities. It became fun to notice so much about my matches. This sense of curiosity made each date exciting just for the many things I could learn from each woman I sat across from. I noticed the quirky and the quality in their personalities. I picked up on subtle non-verbal cues and noted their manner of dress, how they carried themselves and how they listened and responded to me in our short time together.

Well ahead of a coffee date, I noticed the quality of communication as well. How quickly would she respond to my messages? If we spoke on the phone, how engaged was I? Was she engaged in the conversation too? The information came both from my own sensations and what I was experiencing of her. Sometimes it got a little crazy trying to keep track of everyone, but even THAT became data for me. If I was having a hard time remembering, it might mean they were not very memorable. Especially when I had multiple dates in a single day.

Don't Try This At Home

Occasionally I would book as many as 4 dates in one day. I would setup to work from a nearby cafe and invite my matches to 8am, lunchtime, and afternoon/evening dates for a cup of tea or light meal. I learned as I went along that this actually served me well by lowering the expectation to be perfect. My dates would walk into the cafe with work clothes on and I could see them at various stages of their day. Again, I was interested in authenticity more than how she presented.

I realize this level of dating frequency isn't accessible for everyone. To that I say, make this experience your own. You don't have to have 100 dates in 100 days to get the experience I've had. You can create your own dating experiment that fits into your schedule.

Question: How did I handle 2nd & 3rd dates?

After roughly 70 dates I felt that I was nearing a point of shifting from dating the many to dating the few. The best way for me to describe it is that I was yearning to delve deeper with a smaller group of matches. I was following – and trusting – all of the sensations and intuitions I'd experienced over the last couple of months. Soon I was out on second dates with 6 women and putting myself "out there" yet again.

This time my dates extended well into an hour or more, as I wanted to tell more of my story and hear more of theirs. I still kept these dates in cafes and tried my best to avoid restaurants – too loud and too many interruptions from the waitstaff. These encounters were much more intimate, and the sharing was rich. This was the kind of dating I longed to experience.

Every woman had her own strengths, talents and flaws of course, but the theme I noticed was how these ladies met me at my emotional and intellectual level. In the past, I'd always felt that I'd dated women who looked up to me and I didn't know how to get out of that pattern. As a result of this approach, I placed myself in meaningful conversations with attractive, powerful women every week!

Question: Did you date people from other races?
  Me: Yes, but no.

If you subscribe to the invention called "race," then yes, but no... I don't find that model of human categorization useful, and it has wreaked havoc on our world in every area of our existence. Yes, the idea of race is at the root of the worldview known as racism, but the idea of race is based on literally nothing. The world has believed a lie – but we have a choice as to whether we endorse or encourage that illusion and the perpetuate the pervasive systemic havoc one little idea has wrought.

It has also created an immense perception of scarcity in dating where no such scarcity actually exists.

In my dating experience, I've matched with, talked with or dated women across many cultures: Indian, Cuban, African,

African-American, Chinese, Haitian, Trinidadian, Dominican, Irish, Italian, Korean and Native American, just to name a few. I've been out with women of all heights and sizes and hair styles from bald to afro to hip-length curls.

This was on purpose. I eliminated my filters.

I looked over my relationship history and realized I'd had very little exposure to women of other cultures. Being the grandson of a German woman and a West African man, I decided that I wanted to be as inclusive as I could be. That meant removing my filters based on someone's involuntary placement on the skin color spectrum and any other identifier.

The more we persist in requiring that we find a match who also matches our skin tone or cultural heritage, the more scarcity we will volunteer ourselves to. For me, this was not an ideal place to begin dating from. Just as I've grown and become more worldly through my travels beyond North America, we grow when we embrace and enjoy the differences among us. Even if there's no romance between us, we can uncover ways to expand our hearts and minds through a vulnerable conversation with a devoted woman of Islam, a agnostic yogi on Chicago's Southside, a Nigerian screenwriter, a Japanese elementary school teacher or the islander who celebrates Carnival each year.

I'm not saying not to honor your values, do that. You SHOULD question any value that isn't based upon personal experience over time. One experience with one person doesn't translate to every person of similar traits. Open those filters and see how abundant the possibilities are.

CHAPTER EIGHTEEN

Let Go of the Outcomes

"Never have your happiness dependent on a yes or no decision from one person."
— James Altucher

I'd swiped right on thousands of women, and matched with upwards of 500 across all of the apps and sites I was on. That's a lot of swiping. I also met quite a few matches offline at events, parties and business functions. As I kept meeting and learning from these ladies, it became clearer to me that those who were sincerely interested stayed in the picture longer. Eventually, the experiences and the information were filtering my possibilities in a very organic way. I kept a calendar for my dates, but didn't keep a spreadsheet or any form of tracking. I just let the stronger connections choose themselves. I made some diehard friends along the way.

A common experience was an inner conversation that kept driving me to predict the outcome of the next date. Something within me was trying to anticipate rejection or disappointment and nudge me to cancel or bail out of the encounter.

Have you ever felt this way?

I began to understand the this was my way of resurrecting the old model of dating, that was all about winning and getting the prize of a Yes. When all that matters is getting a Yes, then reducing the possibility of a No becomes a strategy. I suspect this is the core driver of the phenomenon of ghosting—the abandonment of a match before I can be abandoned by them.

There are other ways to unhook yourself from the outcome of your dating experience

Stay Within Your Means

I made plenty of mistakes. In my swiping I neglected to consider factors like distance and accessibility. Ironically, it seems easier to travel across the country to meet someone than it is to sit in Chicago traffic for two hrs trying to get to a date. One match that I REALLY wanted to meet lived far out in the burbs. This disrupted my work day beyond my level of comfort, and when I realized this coffee date was going to take three hours out of my day and demand some juggling of my schedule, the costs became too high and I called to cancel. Hooked by her intellect and her beauty, I ignored this very obvious data and tried to meet with her again, and again had to cancel. This time she was the one with the feedback—"You've done this twice, I'm out" were her exact words. Ouch. It was well deserved. I wasn't listening to myself and I was disrespecting her time.

Early on my dates were more traditional—longer, more expensive and sometimes exhausting depending on how engaging the person was. I noticed that if I gave a lot of time up front, I felt almost obligated to go out again. This awareness is what prompted me to move to more natural, in-the-moment, casual meetups vs full-out evenings on the town. The lower the whole cost of the early dates, the more I could invest my authenticity without a fear of loss. Combining my approach of early transparency and applying the Relatabilities, to be covered in the next section, the outcome of each experience was that I had a brief but intimate conversation with someone who I may or may not want to speak with again. I'd been unhooked.

Over-investing your time, energy and money into the dating experience is a sure path to being hooked on outcomes. You'll want a return on those investments and perhaps this will drive decisions that you wouldn't have made apart from your "sunk costs." Stay within your means and your current reality. There is no scarcity except in our belief.

Keep it Moving

I realize there are many folks who have a hard time meeting people "too soon" or prefer chatting on the app a long time before breaking the digital barrier. I'd declared openly in my profile that I wasn't like that—that I wanted to meet and talk. I was ready! If a match didn't reciprocate I kindly honored that in my response and then I unmatched them. I was ready, and if the women who swiped right on me weren't equally ready, that was enough information for me to keep it moving.

Baller was a bright personality who brought fun and interesting conversation and presence to our coffee date. We planned to meet again, but only managed a few text exchanges and she cancelled over and over again. After the second cancel I simply let it go. The moment I sensed that I was working too hard to connect, I knew it was time to move on. Hope and change are not a dating mindset. I don't know what she was dealing with at the time, but it clearly wasn't time for us to connect. Keep it moving.

Don't do this alone

You might think these pitfalls and mistakes were bringing me down. To the contrary, the experiences brought such a flow of aliveness and curiosity that I couldn't wait to see what would happen next! I was having regular check-in calls with Joe and he often helped me sift through each date with his signature candor and non-PC insights. Like I said before, everyone needs a Joe. See my website for more resources, webinars and Q&A sessions where you can get your concerns and challenges addressed. You're not alone in this.

Date more people, more often, with greater curiosity and realistic expectations. Learn from everything. Let go of the outcomes.

Part 2: On Loving

CHAPTER NINETEEN
Who Taught You How to Love?

Someone taught me how to love.

For the majority of our young lives, we are subject to the ways of our culture, family of origin when it comes to how we think and act on matters of the heart. As a species, humans have evolved beyond the primal fundamentals of expanding the tribe and mere survival as a reason for mating. Yet, those reasons are still at the core of most parental angst about making sure their sons and daughters get married and have children of their own.

But at some point in our adulthood, we have a choice to either sustain those beliefs about relationships or we begin to question and even challenge those ideas.

I say, let's question everything. Many of our relationship practices are based on cultures and ideologies originating thousands of years ago. If we could think differently about how we relate to each other in this information-overload era, what would love look like?

So, who taught you how to love?

Here's a few conversation starters:

- How do you define Love? Relationship? Romance? Monogamy?
- What would your family not approve of in a partner? Why? Does that matter to you?
- How does your experience of love and romantic relationship compare to others in your circle of friends? What's different? Similar?
- What feeds your soul? What nourishes you?

Why am I asking these questions? The lineage of our current relationship mental model is important to understand if we're going to create entirely new models going forward.

In my family, there was a pattern of emotional and physical abuse within marriages. I distinctly remember trying to break up a fight between my mom and dad by throwing a pillow at them as they fought. These repeated experienced shaped my thinking about how two people "in-love" are supposed to relate to each other. I made up my mind back then that I wouldn't have that kind of experience. So I went to the extreme side of that and became the nicest guy I could muster. Of course, this led to several relationships where I was the last to know a relationship was over because I was so conflict-avoidant that I shunned the conversations that would've made the relationships last longer than they did.

My mental model was to lay low, stay under the radar and steer clear of conflict. It made me feel safe, but it wasn't a loving model for relationship. In my childhood, this was a self-protecting decision, but in adulthood it became a habit—a choice by way of habit.

When we choose safety instead of vulnerability, we deny ourselves the giving AND receiving of nourishment that love is. Love IS nourishment.

Our upbringing shapes our capacity and capability to give and receive the nourishment called love. It shapes our Partner Vision. It shapes our judgment of how nourishment feels. Period.

Be curious when you hear yourself defending your way of being in a relationship by saying things like, "this is just the way I am." It may be the way you were trained to be, it might be the a mirror of the environment you grew up in—but it is not entirely you. Your model for relationships may be a reflection of the manner of nourishment you learned in your childhood, but is now no longer useful in supporting the quality of nourishment in relationship you desire today. In fact, it may be the very thing keeping more love flowing into your life.

So question everything.

You can unlearn the learning of your childhood. You can reinvent your relationships by learning new thoughts and habits along with fortifying the values that have led you here. Teach yourself how to love in the here and now—not based on your past. Only you know what nourishes you. It's a far more nourishing experience for your partner, when you know how to nourish (and love) yourself well.

CHAPTER TWENTY
Developing Your RelatAbilities™

During a 10-day Vipassana meditation retreat in Southern California, I reflected on my dating journey and the contents of this book that had already been written. I began to form a set of principles that wove a thread throughout my dating experience—I call them RelatAbilities™. You may notice some familiar ideas, and there will also be some ideas that will require some open-mindedness to engage with them. That's ok. I don't expect this approach to sit easy with anyone. It stretched me. There were times when I simply didn't want to do it this way - and those times that I didn't apply this approach felt like hitting the rumble strips on the side of the road late at night.

It woke me up.

Each principle encourages you to see yourself and your date through a distinct lens that may reveal something about you or your date that you can use to determine whether someone is a good fit for you or not. Each principle calls you to greater self-leadership in not just your love life, but across all of your relationships.

The RelatAbilities™ are opportunities to integrate unique

qualities to your way of being. Each principle invites a level of awareness that not only improves the quality of your dating and relationship life but also may serve to increase your capacity in every area of your life. Many of my family, friends and colleagues have already begun to express how practicing these principles has begun to open up new possibilities in their marriages, friendships and careers.

I invite you to those same possibilities.

CHAPTER TWENTY-ONE
Invitation

> "We live between the act of awakening and the act of surrender."
> – John O'Donohue

RelatAbility #1: Invitation

"I accept Life's invitation to become more of myself each day. I breathe in the possibilities of expansion and abundance in every dimension of my life. I answer the call to know myself, to know my effect on others and my impact in the world. I am open to experience. I live in this moment. I am increasing the trust I have in myself and all of my faculties of mind, body and spirit. I express my emotions fully and freely, as I daily move toward a more inclusive, well-traveled and loving way of living."

This is a foundational step in your journey. You are figuring out how ready you really are. Your heart and mind may be at odds. Heart may be saying that you deserve to be with someone special, while Mind is saying your credit sucks and you're living with your parents. Be aware that when you decide on any direction, there will be outside voices speaking to your choice as well. How you respond to those voices and honor your own will add to the information you're learning about yourself. The invitation is an exploration of anything that keeps you from being 100% you. Emotional baggage, trauma, unfinished business in your relationships, finances and family – these all weigh in during this principle.

It's important that we make distinctions between what we want in the moment, and what we are ready for. We may desire a relationship, but our economic, emotional or physical condition simply can't bear the weight of another person in our lives. Is the invitation drawing you to personal stability? Work on that. Are you struggling with low self-esteem? Work in that space. This breath is about your ability to hear the call toward breaking your boundaries – enlarging your realm of influence.

It's critical to every relationship you affect, that you know how ready and able you are to contribute to a healthy, growing relationship – and hopefully, you want to meet someone who is doing the same kind of self-study. For me, there was nothing more frustrating than sitting across from someone who had no curiosity about themselves or the world they live in.

So when you hear this call to becoming – this breath of invitation – honor the direction to work on your inner relationship, or to launch into a journey toward connection with someone else. This is the inward call to readiness for a relationship. This is the call to a heroic journey toward love.

You may experience this in the form of a yearning to be connected, to experience greater intimacy. A counterfeit of this yearning is a more primal drive to experience safety and to be touched. Don't confuse these.

What are you inviting others to? Drama? Baggage? To be a bandage for your emotional wounds? There's a choice we make in this moment, to deal with our pain or keep playing through it —we pay a price for playing through—and we make others pay for it too.

I met Bella at a small bar after chatting and a few phone conversations. I was early in my experiment and I wasn't asking many questions in those pre calls that would filter for certain situations. I found out she was still married but living apart for a number of years and delaying divorce. I've been there, so I was open to getting to know her anyway. Our exchanges became intense discussions about hurt, transition and letting go. Over the summer we talked off and on and it became clear that we weren't a good fit for romance, but the respect and honesty was such a gift. We both accepted the invitation, even though the invitation didn't lead to love - it did lead to friendship. I think we both were a bit more "ready" for whatever was coming next.

In this encounter, I realized the importance of being clear about my invitation. In every exchange, I am hosting another human being in my presence. What am I inviting my guest to? What kind of a host am I being in the moment? Am I creating a space that she wants to spend her time in? Is the space I'm creating healthy? nourishing? alive? engaging? It's interesting to hear friends discuss their dating experiences as if we don't have a role to play for the space that we create for each other. The time, location, privacy and ambiance of the space we choose to invite others to may have deep impact on the quality of your experience. Take the time to curate your encounters.

If you're not ready to increase the quality of life for another human being; if you're not able to add value in some meaningful way, grow yourself up before stepping into someone's life. Ask yourself the question: What am I inviting another person into?

You can only answer this question if you've done some of your own work and you've developed some level of self awareness. begin to take small, meaningful actions to make new habits and behaviors that support the kind of person you want to become. A key part of the principle of invitation is moving away from who you are not, and toward who you are becoming. The invitation is to be more you, know your value and assess your readiness for relationship. Take the time.

Your Assignment:

1) Reflect on who you were a year ago, and who you are today.
2) Who are you becoming?
3) What influences are shaping you?
4) Which influences would you keep or eject from your life?
5) What new influences would you like to have in your life?

CHAPTER TWENTY-TWO
Commitment

"He had to choose between something he had become accustomed to and something he wanted to have."
— Paulo Coelho, The Alchemist

RelatAbility #2: Commitment

"I am committed to moving forward: forward toward the best in me. I am committed to the lifelong experiment of being. The laboratory is my life and every encounter is alchemy. I commit to observing the results of this chemistry with self-love in mind. I commit to contribute to such experiences, more than I consume them. I commit to my own emotional and physical safety, and remove myself from conditions that present a threat to my wellbeing. I commit to reflecting on whether those threats are real or imagined. I freely present my whole self and commit to revealing who I am, more and more each day."

This is about your ability to persist in the face of disappointment and difficulty.

There were many times when my hundred day journey made me want to give up. After four dates in a single day and being frustrated by the quality of interactions, it would've been easy for me to blame those experiences on the women sitting across from me. But the more I experienced those kinds of dates, the more I saw how I was showing up, how inauthentic I may have been coming across. This was cause for reflection and adjustment on my part, not abandoning the experiment. It was also a reminder for me to stay on my own side, to go through this process and not quit on myself. I began to ask myself better questions: How was I creating these experiences? How was I contributing? It was this kind of reflection that kept me learning and moving forward.

On my wall of shame is a group I'll call The Bench, representing experiences that made me wish I'd never started the dating adventure. One match talked about how much she hated her job for an hour, never asking me a single question. Another woman spoke very highly of her father – nothing wrong with that – except we were on a date and I couldn't get a word or question in anywhere. I could form a women's basketball team with a deep bench from the ladies who were actually still in some form of relationship or "situationship." How was I contributing to this pattern?

Even the best plans can be disrupted by the unexpected. I got ghosted several times. I went to locations and dates didn't show up. I'm sure I've ghosted a few over the years. Still, I persisted. The lessons poured in. I needed to stay in this experience long enough to maximize my learning.

Decide to be open to the experience. Commit to exposing yourself to more of humanity in your dating adventure. This is not about finding the mythical "one," but more about expanding your world through many small moments that build over time. Commit to being authentic and present, so you and your dates can learn and grow from each encounter. To be clear, this is not about finding someone at this stage, as Allen Iverson famously said: it's practice.

I've always believed that if I place myself in the path of opportunities, opportunities will "miraculously" cross my path. Remember, your comfort zone keeps you exactly where you are and it's designed to make it hard for you to break your self-imposed gravity. You will need to repeatedly choose to EXPAND that comfort zone in order to live a different quality of life. What are you willing to be committed to?

Your Assignment:
1) What are your quitting points?
2) Where do you consistently find yourself retreating from what you want?
3) Reflect on how you've historically kept commitments.
4) What relationship comfort zone needs to be expanded?

CHAPTER TWENTY-THREE

Curiosity

> "The important thing is not to stop questioning. Curiosity has its own reason for existence."
> – Albert Einstein, TIME Magazine

RelatAbility #3: Curiosity

> "I wonder at the world around me. Each experience holds a mystery to be explored and answers to be revealed. We each experience a day apart and return to each other changed and undiscovered. We are never the same person. How curious can I be toward another human? How do I clean the slate and offer wide eyes and open ears to another soul? How much do I long for someone to be so curious about me?"

This breath calls us to suspend our judgments, ask questions that create intimacy and respect the daily possibility of change.

From the moment we see someone of interest, our unconscious biases kick in and work to protect us from both real and imagined threats. How we pay attention to these judgments as they show up, is critical to our vetting process. In the early days of summer I was mixing my old dating pattern with my new ideas, and getting mixed results. I was swiping right on my stereotypical "types" and trying to put my "best foot forward," and mostly putting my foot in my mouth trying to be memorable and impressive. I would have a chat with a match, set up a phone call, talk with her and that would be the end. No date. No second call. Not even an ongoing chat. I wasn't paying attention to the clues the ladies were giving me, nor was I honoring my gut reactions to each one I spoke to. I was shopping while thirsty, hungry AND unaware. It was a bad look for me. Anytime you try to merge your old mindset with something new, you're bound to re-create old results.

A breakthrough came after I matched with Brilliant, a researcher at a university. After a brief exchange, we decided to meet face to face. She was a deep thinker compared to previous dates, and our conversation moved well past my usual 30 minute limit. Something about her own intellectual curiosity sparked curiosity in me too! I noticed a shift in my own awareness. I was downloading a ton of data from her AND my own experience of the date. She was engaging, but often preoccupied, which I assumed could be related to her child at home with a sitter. I enjoyed hearing her social justice orientation and the sage, grey streak of hair she kept flipping back—a cue of interest for me to take in. I had a moment of clarity as I found out her child was just entering school age years. I felt that this wasn't a good fit for me, and even though her attractiveness and intellect were unquestionable, I didn't want to mislead her. This date opened my eyes to the possibilities of the micro-date, and to integrating my sensory data into my dating experience. She also opened me up to dating women who matched me mentally and spiritually. This was intentionally denying my intellectual superiority streak and staying open to every experience. Brilliant helped me ground my future dates in that experience of mutual intellectual stimulation.

I found that the path of least resistance for me was to date those who looked up to me in some way. There's nothing inherently wrong with being looked up to, but if I notice a pattern of this, the principle of curiosity says it's worth looking into. Our hearts like to form protective strategies that keep us from being vulnerable. By choosing to date only those who look up to or admire me in some way, I may be avoiding the challenge of a strong woman who is on equal footing with me. Ancient scriptures describe this as being "equally yoked," referring to a farming practice of plowing hard ground with oxen of the same size and strength. If a farmer were to use oxen of different sizes and capabilities, they would have a harder time working together.

I don't want to spend too much time discussing farming and oxen. I hope you get the idea.

If you are prone to dating the same type of person, here's an opportunity to catch yourself in the act. Are we filtering out good prospects because of some pre-judging? Are we limiting our field of relationship possibilities because of some cultural mandate, religious restriction, even the amount of melanin in one's skin? Are we really that shallow and short-sighted?

Question those assumptions.

How wonderfully ironic would it be, if the most fitting lover for you, also has traits that you have been conditioned to avoid? They may have qualities that will cause you to grow emotionally and culturally. What experiences do you historically run from? What age groups? What skin tones? Curiosity allows you to playfully explore possibilities that you may have overlooked in the past. You never know what Love will look like when it presents itself. Don't let your home training blind you from what's possible. Maintain a state of awe. Your boat wasn't built to stay in the harbor. Get out into the ocean and explore. Stay curious.

Your Assignment:
1) What limits have you placed on your dating experience?
2) What unspoken rules have you held onto from your upbringing and parental expectations?
3) Do they still apply to you today, or are you simply doing what you were taught to do?
4) Take time to reflect on how removing those limitations would change your experience.

CHAPTER TWENTY-FOUR
Engagement

> "Wearing a mask wears you out. Faking it is fatiguing. The most exhausting activity is pretending to be what you know you aren't."
> – Rick Warren

RelatAbility #4: Engagement

> "I answer this call to be fully present with each human encounter. I breathe in focus and breathe out distractions. With each encounter, each engagement, each exposure of my heart, I will build my awareness of my identity, my value and my power."

The principle of engagement calls upon us to remove the distractions, masks and armor so that we can connect deeply with another human being. No matter the setting, take the time to consider all of the possible distractions from your conversation, video chat, or face-to-face meeting. Wherever possible leave your devices away from your person or turned off. For added effect, announce that you're doing so. This reinforces your commitment to being fully engaged with your date, and simultaneously invites them to do the same.

The next thing that the principle of engagement calls us to, is to deeply listen. It's one thing to hear the person across the table, it's a very different thing to listen. Hearing requires no effort and can be done passively. Listening is an intentional act.

One of the hardest things to resist is the desire to form questions while you're listening. Instead of yielding to this temptation, save your question formation until the person has stopped talking. Make sure they know that you have heard them and mention some things that stood out for you. Most people go through an entire day and never receive the gift of being heard. Even if this date ends up going nowhere, you have the beautiful opportunity to hear someone.

You've moved from being fully present, to listening deeply, to a place of inquiry and dialogue. It all happens much faster than this of course, but this is why it's so important to have these breaths in mind ahead of each encounter. The more you practice, the more of a habit you've built, and these practices become second nature. Now, this practice calls us to draw from our listening work and ask questions that reflect our interest in another human being.

The opposite of engagement is withdrawal. This shows up as distancing, evasiveness and possibly even the dating phenomenon of "ghosting," or unexplained disappearance of a dating prospect. I'll bundle each of these withdrawal clues into a single word – let's call them masks.

Bistro was a flurry of energy and the life of the party. She was also deeply passionate about the annual Trinidad & Tobago

Carnival, where she donned elaborate masks and scant outfits to parade through the city. Lots of data to think about in that sentence alone.

After a micro-date and a fun outing to a show, I began to notice a very dark and lonely side to her that she tried very hard to conceal. She was a very successful professional, but she was managing a personal life filled with purely transactional relationships. I'd told her everything about me, yet I still knew very little about her family and background. She wasn't engaging me equally, and it was starting to hurt. She began wrestling with relocation overseas for a new job. We began to find it difficult to stay connected when we were both on the road for work. After we both returned from a long stint without contact, we met for dinner and honestly shared our concerns about what was happening. We never spoke again after that evening. Later I thought about the paradox of how she could reveal herself in a physical manner in front of thousands, but remain emotionally armored while we were dating—and again, how had I contributed to that?

We all wear masks throughout our lives, and in different environments we feel safe enough to let our masks come off - this is one way to describe authenticity - the removal of our mask. Vulnerability, in contrast, is the skill of keeping the mask off for longer durations of time and in more areas of our lives. When dating, I think we create the conditions for mutual deception when we begin our dates with masks on. We are both inauthentic AND invulnerable at a time when we are supposed to be trying to get to know each other. You'll find that as your confidence grows (and it will as your date count increases) you'll find yourself removing your mask faster and keeping it off longer - resulting in greater date experiences as you give your date permission to join you in that higher level of engagement. Proof of engagement is that you know more about someone once you've left their presence.

I want you to notice when you're withdrawing to your masks, and ask yourself why.

Masks exist because they serve a purpose – to protect us from pain and rejection. Even the most authentic person you know can pull out a mask when they need one. On your dating journey, make sure you notice when you put your mask back on, and when your date does the same. These aren't causes for judgment, just sources of information on how to relate to that person. It's all a part of being fully engaged in those moments, and catching the many ways that we try to dis-engage in order to remain safe or avoid being fully seen by another person. Those who join you in such sharing have accepted your invitation to see you, and to be seen. This is excellent data for you to assess whether pursuing another date with this person is a good idea.

Your authenticity and vulnerability may not be met with an equal response. This too, is data for you to take in and add to your learning. Those who are unwilling to engage with you are telling you exactly how they may be in a relationship. Each encounter, each engagement, each exposure of your heart will build your awareness of your identity, your value and your power.

So, engage.

Your Assignment:
1) How can you spend more time unmasked?
2) What feelings arise when you think about becoming more vulnerable?
3) What are your go-to distractions to avoid deep discussions, silence or disagreement?

CHAPTER TWENTY-FIVE
Non-Attachment

> "As a water bead on a lotus leaf, as water on a red lily, does not adhere, so the sage does not adhere to the seen, the heard, or the sensed."
> –The Buddha

RelatAbility #5: Equanimity

> "I see the world as it is. I see people as they are. I see myself as I am. The polarity is real, and I am a part of it. I have the same capacity to blindly love and blindly hate as any other human, yet I stay aware that these emotions come and go. I am not attached to them. I can experience the love and the hate equally, but not become addicted to either. I am alive, but no single experience is my master."

This is about your ability to fully experience someone or something, and still let it go.

Having over 100 dates gave me a unique perspective on letting go. There were matches that I didn't want to ever talk to again.

There were those whom I would lovingly support until the end of time. That's how wide a range of experience I've had. What I came to know for myself was this paradox: I yearn for attachment, yet for me to be fully present with my match, I also needed to hold a non-attachment to my perceptions, judgments, aversions and cravings. How else could I learn something new with each encounter? How could I curiously see my match as a new person every time we meet?

Our Hollywood mindset around dating has set many of us up to suffer. Our expectations are so high, so unrealistic, yet so deeply held and unquestioned, that anyone who swipes right on us has a massive mountain of expectation to climb before we accurately see them. Despite the malaise, there are bright moments to offer.

I was driving through Grant Park in Chicago when my Tinder notification went off. Sitting at a stop light, I checked the app and saw British. She'd already started a chat with me. Within minutes I'd pulled over and had a full discussion and decided to meet for lunch. There was a catch though – she asked me to bring her a sandwich. While this was odd, I shrugged and agreed! This felt like an adventure, so I was all in. She was staying at a boutique hotel and asked me to meet her there. Now, I don't advise doing this, but for some reason it just felt ok with me and I grabbed a couple of sandwiches and walked into her lobby. I called her and she tested my courage once again – "Come up to my room."

I'm not crazy, just open-minded (insert sly grin). I got to her floor and noticed a guy cleaning a room nearby. I asked him to watch and listen as I went in, and if he heard anything odd to call for help! She opened the door and invited me in as she wiped her nose and sniffled, thanking me for trusting her invitation.

We had our sandwiches, she made tea, and we talked for 3 hours about dating, life and love. Her voice reminded me of Downtown Julie Brown from MTV in the 80s. Time flew by, and though I wanted to get to know her better, it turns out that she was a flight attendant leaving for the UK the next morning. We shared a deep hug and said goodbye, and never spoke again.

That totally unplanned encounter taught me a powerful lesson. British was evidence to me that I could let go of something really amazing; that I could take risks and enjoy the moment. This happened many times over. I could have chosen to internally suffer over meeting women like her and not being able to pursue more, but instead I let them go in my heart.

Suffering is the result of some type of attachment. In dating, often the suffering is the result of becoming attached to a desired outcome or an emotional state that you crave. You may be holding on to experiences from a past relationship and now you're suffering because you expect your new prospects to live up to that same experience. That's not fair to you or your matches.

With each encounter, between each encounter, take the time to release your expectations. Release the last date from your mind and bring yourself into the present moment. Open up to experience the person across from you without the "ghosts of lovers past" haunting your exchange. If you meet someone outstanding, could you walk away with just the encounter and still be okay? That's a sign of emotional fitness.

When we practice non-attachment, we are not suppressing our enjoyment of life. In fact, we can enjoy the moment with great appreciation, and then we are in the next moment experiencing it wholly, without craving a return to the previous moment.

Everyday Dating provide a perfect playground to practice this. As you meet each prospect, enjoy the moment! Recall what you enjoyed and what you learned in that experience. As you have another date, experience it as a new encounter. Deny the urge to recreate the last experience. Resist your efforts to avoid the bad experiences of previous dating encounters. Just be in the experience.

Your Assignment:

1) Reflect on your ability to enjoy the moment. Light a small candle and observe it for 3 minutes. Notice where your mind takes you. Can you enjoy the flame moment to moment? How quickly are you distracted?

2) Take inventory of the beautiful things in your life. How attached are you to them? What emotions arise as you consider letting any of these people, things or experiences exit your life?

CHAPTER TWENTY-SIX
Freedom

"Liberty means responsibility. That is why most men dread it."
— George Bernard Shaw, Man & Superman

RelatAbility #6: Freedom

> "I am free. I live and move and have my being in this freedom. I'm free to follow my yearnings and enjoy the experience of being and becoming a more aware, loving human. I'm free from societal constructs that attempt to dictate who I "should" love, or what I "should" do, be or have. I'm free to walk away from experiences that dull or constrain the expression of my authenticity. Yet, I am equally free to create as I am to destroy; free to build up and to tear down; to nourish and to starve; to extend relationship and to withhold it. My freedom has consequences, and I own them all."

When was the last time you were entirely responsible for your own fulfillment when dating?

This is a form of freedom. This is about your ability to assert your will and create your own experience of the world.

When you're meeting someone new, you have the power to say what you want. Be explicit about how you want someone to treat you. Clearly communicate your standards and your intentions.

I went so far as to state in my profile," I'm looking to friend you first, not the other F-word." This served as an upfront way to bring the unspoken assumptions forward into the discussion. Some women gave me feedback that they thought that statement came across as insincere, while most others enjoyed my candid humor. This was an intentional filter. If someone was offended by those words, that's okay – it was their reaction and that in itself was data for me. I was more interested in those who accurately saw me as being honest.

By exercising my freedom, I polarized a few women who may have otherwise been strong prospects. This is a form of freedom. You are free to craft a profile that offends some, while it filters for a few great people. If you're on a date and your match seems inattentive, you are free to point that out and give them feedback on your experience.

I told Brunch that her phone was a distraction for me and asked her to put it away for the remainder of our date. Again, if you can't give me 20-30 minutes of your undivided attention, the likelihood of that improving when we're in a relationship is quite low. She struggled with wanting to check her phone every three minutes, and by the end of our date, I told her that she seemed to be a friendly person, but that I just wasn't interested because it appeared that she wasn't very interested either.

That may seem harsh, but I think that kind of candid feedback can make everyone's dating experience richer. Tell people your truth. Say what you want from each other. Let someone know how their words and behavior have affected you. Perhaps my date was a single mother and was checking on her child – sharing that would have deepened our conversation since I'm also a father. I make sure I put things like that in my profile because it becomes a filter. I realize that women avoid disclosing this information, but really, if a guy swipes left because you have a kid, did you REALLY want to meet him? I feel you. It's hard sometimes, because we naturally want to be likable, but there comes a time when the price of being likable is too damn high.

Freedom has consequences. The consequences can save you hours of dating frustration, and perhaps more importantly, years of relationship struggle – all because you exercised your freedom to challenge; to move on; to get up and leave the table.

You may feel obligated to say yes when you really want to say no. Honor that nudge to stand up for yourself. The consequence is that you've taught yourself how you want to be treated, and taught someone else too. You. Are. Free.

Your Assignment:
1) Say "no" more this week.
2) Use "no" to set boundaries for yourself.
3) Become a "no" artist and be your own advocate.
4) Protect your time, energy and creativity by saying "no" more.

CHAPTER TWENTY-SEVEN
Choice

> "Don't ask yourself what the world needs,
> ask yourself what makes you come alive
> & then go do it. Because what the world needs is people who
> have come alive."
> –Howard Thurman

RelatAbility #7: Choice

"I choose to honor my body, mind and spirit in and through my relationships. I choose to grow relationships that increase both my capacity and empathy. I choose to use my power and influence to leave others enriched from our time together. I choose to feed my mind with the ingredients that will produce quality decisions. I choose to confront my inner saboteur, victim, child and opportunist—they are my shadows and I choose to embrace them as part of me and hear their voices. I choose to love myself first; to stay on my own side; to show up and play full out in every interaction. I always have this power to choose."

Freedom is not the same thing as Choice. When you choose, you are exercising your freedom as you eliminate the options in front of you. The principle of choice brings in your creative power to follow your yearnings and honor what makes you come alive. We have this power to move in the direction of either aliveness or atrophy – growth or decline. We can put our freedom to use and declare that we choose our own satisfaction and happiness, in order to bring those qualities into every relationship and every encounter.

Sometimes, we aren't the chosen one.

Near the end of my dating spree, I'd narrowed my matches down to 3 inspiring women. They all knew I was dating others and I knew they were doing the same. I'd met Brilliant through a mutual friend and over time developed a deep respect for her intellect, creativity and hustle. One day I sent her a text to see if she was free to join me at a party later that week. She replied with, " Yes….with my BF… a lot can happen in a week right?"

Practicing both non-attachment and choice, I simply and honestly congratulated her on her new relationship. There was nothing but love there. Love is always a choice no matter what the level of expression.

Choice is, in a strange way, terrifying. It is the very expression of our power and freedom. We consider cutting off our various options and may lose access to something we moderately enjoyed or perhaps had become comfortable with. We could make a wrong choice.

Applied to dating, choice calls upon us to be responsible for our satisfaction, continue with relationships that increase our aliveness and experience, and separate from relationships that don't nurture us or just aren't making us come alive.

Of course, this is YOUR choice. No one will make it for you. No one else has to live with your choices. So, choose well.

Your Assignment:
1) Choose to have more of what inspires and feeds your soul enter into your life.
2) Choose to nourish your body and mind.
3) Choose to reinvent your living space, personal style and ask more from your relationships.

CHAPTER TWENTY-EIGHT
Shift the Intimacy Inward

"The sacred and the sensual are inseparable. Only in humans do we separate the elements and suffer in our repression. Flowers shine and animals face the sun but humans hide themselves from the light."
– Lizz Wright

Shift the Intimacy Inward

The intention behind my own dating experience was to meet more women and get to know myself along the way.

Sex came up every now and then.

I realized that if I was really interested in knowing myself, injecting sex in my early conversations would distract me from getting to know the person and them getting to know me. Putting out that kind of energy invites your match to assume that's what you want - even if it's not what you express that you want.

I committed to a guideline that I would only consider physical intimacy three to four dates into the experience, and even then, it would be measured. Intimacy is a sacred space that can easily be destroyed by reckless action. If you want intimacy beyond the physical realm, invest in building emotional intimacy instead. Explore an emerging relationship from the heart first and let the body be the final frontier. Even though I was explicit about my intentions, I still occasionally got the feedback that it seemed like I wasn't interested in them "that way." That's data.

In my mind, I took that as a clue that she may have been running out of vulnerability to give, and sex may have been the only thing she felt she had left to offer. This may or may not have been true—but I wonder if there isn't some old learning about how a man "should' be that' influencing how you're receiving a person as they are. Do men want sex? On a primal level, I'd say yes, of course. From my conversations with women of many orientations and cultures, the same is true. Did you buy this book because you wanted sex?

I'mma leave that right there for you to think about.

Sex is easy. The mechanics are obvious. The outcome is predictable.

What we want is love, nourishment, intimacy. Everyone will have their own way of defining these, based on your original relationship model, yet, there's nothing like being fully seen by another human being, emotionally, mentally and yes, physically. But physical intimacy during the dating experience can be a two-edged sword—giving quick intimacy before other forms of intimacy are shared and even creating a mask of intimacy that covers the absence of other expressions. The Hook of Attraction sinks in here. Beware this hook.

Here are three reasons why I suggest leaving sex out of your experience as long as you can do so:

1. Intimacy comes first. When sex is not an option, other sensory paths to intimacy must be developed. For men, we often resort to sex when our words run out, or we begin to feel a need to assert our masculinity through sex. For women, I've noticed that when it seems like the guy is backing away, the woman will place her sexuality into the foreground. This is why the pickup artists use tricks like "negging" to put a woman on the defensive and get her to try to convince them to engage with her. Both responses are rooted in the hook of scarcity. Men, let your words run out, and let the listening begin. Women, if he backs away emotionally, it's either a game, or its data and should spark your curiosity. Your sexual energy is not proof of interest, and it's only one expression of your personal power.

2. Don't cloud your clarity. The longer you can maintain your mental clarity and see the data for what it is, without hooks or rationalizations, the better your choices will become. You'll be able to observe your match's actions and words and note how they align with your values. Having sex too early in a dating relationship is like a throwing a boulder into a pond and expecting the water to stay crystal clear.

3. Sex wasn't meant to be safe. Your quest for love does not demand that you risk your most intimate levels with just anyone. Sex is meant to be a spiritual container of fearless play, exposure, abandon and uninhibited curiosity. Access to your inner world, emotionally and physically, is a gift to be earned through experiences that build trust and mutual respect. (Someone out there might read this as my saying not to practice safe sex….no…wrap it up.)

I'm not going to prescribe a 90-day no-zone or any such nonsense here. You're an adult. It's not the 50's. Here's the reality: if your intention is to have sex and assert your sexual power, that's all good when consensual, but don't expect those hookups to develop into something in the range of your Partner Vision. It's highly unlikely - not impossible, but unlikely - and outside of the design of this approach.

If you know that for you, a basic kiss will lead to groping and grinding, it might be a good idea to refrain from even kissing until you've established emotional and intellectual intimacy. Ignoring this will set you up for those annoying hooks to undermine your clarity.

But by all means, be sensual. As you date your matches, enjoy the process of thoughtful preparation. By the second or third date, you will have good data to apply to how you are interacting and showing them your level of interest. Use that information! One match who I had several dates with told me that she loved a certain kind of flower, so one evening I drove by her place and left a small bouquet for her to enjoy. It was a small gesture of my growing interest and displayed my personal value of chivalry.

Transmute that sexual energy into creative sensuality.

Sensuality is often mistaken as sexuality. Not so. Cooking, making fragrant tea or coffee, wrapping a gift, a drawing, even a custom musical composition can deeply affect the quality of your interactions. These types of gestures are not even available to you until a second or third date as you're still learning the likes and dislikes of your matches.

Do you see how important the data gathering process is?

This approach builds from experience to experience. Take your time. Take sex out of the conversation. Look for inward experiences of intimacy instead.

Assignment:

1) What is your reaction to this chapter?

2) Reflect on what emotions cam up as you read this and what sexuality has meant to you in relationships. Has it been used as a form of power? Negotiation? Punishment? Manipulation? Creativity?

3) How would you like to explore expressing your sensuality as you date?

CHAPTER TWENTY-NINE
Trusting Again

I'm not going to be cliche and write about forgiveness. I think forgiveness is an oversimplification. Try this: completely express your emotions until there's nothing left to express.

Where forgiveness goes wrong, is that we think that by moving quickly to forgiveness, we've handled the matter. In reality, we've issued a verdict without fully giving due process to the pain. IN my experience, and in that of my clients, when you've run out of pain to express and process, forgiveness happens without even saying "i forgive you."

I recently witnessed a couple in the throes of relationship hell. They were fighting for their connection while also fiercely protecting themselves from the other's hurtful words. I noticed that one of them kept shutting down—imposing a rule about controlling their anger perhaps. The second time I observed this, I slammed my hand on the table and said "that's it! That's the anger you want them to see!"

"But when I do that they never respond well"

I responded with, "That's why you practice your anger here, so you both can learn how to express it safely, and see each other's pain."

It wasn't until they saw each other's deep hurt, past the stories, the histories and the betrayals, that they were able to return to their original connection. It takes time.

Learning to trust again is a practice. You don't learn by reading about it. You learn by engaging in small trusting actions, then expanding those actions into larger experiences.

As you build your emotional fitness, you'll begin to see how much more resilient you're becoming. As you meet more people and risk a little more vulnerability each time, you'll discover how quickly you bounce back from those encounter both negative and positive.

This begins with trusting yourself, then trusting in others, then trusting the wider world around you. There are plenty of reasons to withhold trust in this life. But to me, the richness of a relationship happens when I decide to not expect my partner to accept or understand what I choose to reveal. I validate myself as I show my lover who I really am. Suddenly, I'm trusting myself instead of placing that burden on my partner. That is a better foundation. I can always choose to be single again. I'm ok with that.

ASSIGNMENT:
1) What's your current relationship with trust?
2) How does your origin story influence how you trust today?
3) What small actions can you take to increase your trust in your own inner voice?

Part 3: On Being Loved

CHAPTER THIRTY
Receiving What You Asked For

Here's my only sports reference in the entire book: Have you ever seen a football game where the receiver is wide open, the quarterback throws a perfect pass and just as it arrives, the player stumbles, seems surprised by the event, and drops the ball?

I call this phenomenon Dream Shock.

Dream Shock is my word for what happens when a scenario seems too good to be true and one is unprepared for the success. It also happens when we get a new job and feel like we're incompetent or frauds and begin to self-sabotage the opportunity. This happens in love too.

You've been seeing someone for a few months and everything seems to be going VERY well. No drama, no issues. Then something begins to bother you. There MUST be something wrong with this person, right? You become hyperaware and suddenly you're noticing every little nuance of their behavior and monitoring their social media accounts for strange activity. There's no actual cause for suspicion, but your mind is running rampant trying to live up to your relationship model's expectations. You are dropping the ball and failing to receive the experience dropped into your hands.

When we raise our awareness to our relationship model, deny the hook of scarcity and accept the abundance around us, we don't have to be surprised when great things manifest…we can simply be grateful–and hold on to the gift.

You Asked for It, Now Receive It.

Vulnerability. It's the thing I simultaneously crave and fear the most. I don't think I'm alone in that sentiment. I think we all want to be known for who we really are and loved for that authenticity–even despite that authenticity. I don't have to be guarded. I don't need to wear a mask or project a persona for impression's sake–we're way past such things–or so we hope.

There's a deep longing to simply lean into our partner. That longing is tempered by our fear of being used–or even worse–lost in whomever we decide to lean on.

Don't dip your toe into vulnerability, dive in.

The real question is: what does vulnerability look like to you?

I have a few ideas:
- Can I truly be myself in your presence?
- Will you judge me?
- Critique me? Reject me? Exile me?
- Can I think differently from you and engage in discourse without division?
- Can I attempt something risky in your presence without fear of ridicule?
- Can I share my heart and not have it used against me later?

When we are in the process of healing—and we are always healing in some way—it's vital that we see the big picture. When I accept and take in my partner's love, I am answering the same questions for them as well. They are feeling just as exposed; just as afraid; just as unprotected. Accepting is the gift we give to our partners, just as we want to be seen and accepted for who we are.

Vulnerability is the only way to experience life. We try to mitigate our risks. We try to be selectively vulnerable. We do it in business, family and friendships—It doesn't work. It locks out life. After reading hundreds of posts on many social media platforms about love and relationships and living life to the fullest—what I think they are really saying is:

I want to be vulnerable again. I want to be seen.

Yes, there's risk involved in being seen. But isn't that what life is? We take risks, we feel all the feels and we see what happens after we take wise action.

Dr David Schnarch writes about his concept called Self-Validating Intimacy. It is the practice of self-acceptance regardless of the level of acceptance of your partner or anyone else for that matter. What might this look like in your life? You've developed more emotional fitness. You can take a hurt and recover well. Now you bare your soul to another human being and you have already decided that no matter what the response, you're going to be just fine. You may feel fear. You may feel hurt. You will be ok. That's self-validating intimacy. I highly recommend his book, 'The Passionate Marriage" for a deeper, transformative dive into this experience.

Give love. Receive it. Drop the guard and abandon the masks.

When we allow love to affect us, we become the channel for that love to flow through us into others.

Receive what you asked for. It's time for you to get the nourishment you yearn for.

CHAPTER THIRTY-ONE
Choosing Your Groove

Will this work for you? Honestly, it depends.

I saved this tip for last, because I often hear a myriad of excuses for why this approach won't work for someone.

"It works for men but not women."
 "I don't have that kind of time."
 "It might work in [insert big city here] but I'm from [insert small town here]"

None of these excuses really matter. It comes down to the seven RelatAbilities™.

1. Invitation: Explore & evict everything that keeps you from being 100% yourself
2. Commitment: Commit to yourself and your lifelong development
3. Curiosity: Always be learning about yourself and your dates
4. Engagement: Practice your presence
5. Non-Attachment: Unhook yourself from expectations

6. Freedom: Realize you can keep it moving
7. Choice: Keep improving the quality of your choices

But again, can this work for you?

I honestly don't know. What I do know is that I've discussed this model with men and women, young and old, gay and straight – it doesn't seem to affect the level of resonance they have found.

I can't say if you will be as committed as I was to learning about myself after each date. I do know that if I'd given up too soon, I'd still be tolerating less than satisfying relationships.

I don't believe in quick fixes. This will require effort, and you're worth everything you can give to this approach. Yet, there is a possibility that even after taking all of these steps, you may find yourself at a loss for the results you may have been quietly hoping for.

It happened to me.

What I discovered was that even after all of my inner work, there was still another relationship to consider—my relationship with the Universe, or god, or God. Choose your belief. Choose your knowing. I knew that there was still something I needed to release.

Surrender. That was the word that kept sounding in my heart.

Letting go is the key to every single principle. We do this naturally. No one ever taught us how to exhale as newborns. It happens because the body knows that holding that air in will eventually become toxic to the body. When we let the breath go, we are making room for yet another breath that will sustain us.

Exhale. Make room for something great to enter your life.

After you've done all of the work, swiped right, engaged and chosen well, you must let it all go and allow Life to work on your behalf.

Will this work for you? Yes, if you will work it, and surrender.

The magic happens when we choose to take our groove back; when we decide to stop lingering in the hurts of relationships past…and let it all go.

But you don't have to walk this path alone. Share this experience with others, invite them to this process and engage in conversations about how you're growing and learning from the approach. Join me in my live sessions and online course offerings. Practice being present. Build Emotional Fitness together. Choose well. Give yourself the Love you seek.

Thank you for taking this journey with me.

CHAPTER THIRTY-TWO

The Secret of Surrender

"Its just like the water, I ain't felt that way in years"
—Lauryn Hill, MTV Unplugged

My matches dwindled from six matches to three, and suddenly within a span of a week, even those three were becoming questionable. This whole time I'd been practicing non-attachment, and getting better at staying unhooked by the wonderful qualities of each woman I dated.

In the past, I was the common denominator in every failed relationship. This time, I'm still that common thread, but I can tell that I've grown. This time I've been building my emotional fitness. I'm confident, but not arrogant, and I've made some good friends and expanded my professional network. It had been a really great summer.

Truth be told, I had enough data to know that my options were beginning to narrow. I was aware that each of these final three women had qualities I absolutely enjoyed, but none of them embodied the full Vision of A Great Partner I'd been building all along my dating journey. I had a sense that I had yet to meet my vision.

I found myself in exactly the same space as three months earlier, but somehow more open, more available and less filtered. One day I simply surrendered and handed over my dating outcomes to the Universe entirely.

Just a few days later, I was scanning my a social media feed and saw an ad for "a new dating app for Black professionals." This was intriguing, because my experience had prompted me to also consider designing a dating app with precisely the same audience in mind. I installed the app and tinkered around for a while until I'd set up a profile using exactly the same photos and information from my Tinder account. I wasn't looking to launch back into another massive round of dating, but this app was somehow calling me to it.

The next morning I took a few minutes before starting work to browse a few profiles and came across one that instantly caught my attention. She had a beautiful smile, but there was a depth in her eyes that I found compelling. I swiped right, but I wasn't as enthusiastic this time. I went about my work..and almost exactly an hour later, she matched with me and we started a chat that lasted all day, and ended with an invitation from her to Skype later that evening.

We had "dates" by phone or Skype nearly every day from that day forward. She had a tenderness to her voice and a kindness in her eyes. She was naturally sexy, fresh faced and confidently rocked her kinky hair. She knew her power and it oozed from her words and visual presence. We explored our light and our darkness together and committed to an unusual transparency and candor with each other.

I knew she would be an important person in my life from the

very first hello, but let me tell you about the feeling that I began to experience.

Joy – pure joy infused me from head to toe. I hadn't been available to that depth of joy before. I was overwhelmed with light and song and power.

It was as if the ceiling had been ripped away and I was breathing mountain air. I loved the way I felt about myself whenever I was connected to her. I felt her invitation, commitment, curiosity, engagement, non-attachment, freedom and choice in every experience. When we spoke, I heard between her words and felt her heartstrings. Within a few days of conversation I was so taken with her that I felt afraid. I was joyful AND afraid? Wow. We hadn't even met yet. What does that even mean? We had the most spiritual, soul-baring conversations each evening and my friends kept telling me I'd developed an annoying "soul glow."

She lived in Los Angeles. She was what we might call…a baller…(which was a bit intimidating) and my work took me to Southern California on a regular basis. So we planned to meet face-to-face after one of my leadership events. As I caught a ride-share to the brunch spot, my friend Joe sent me a text:

> *Relax. Know that you are today, the manifestation of your investment in your dreams.*
>
> *And as for your present situation, you, a man, are en route to speak with a woman. Period.*
>
> *Woosaaaaah… Be there, be present, and flow…*

His timing was absolutely perfect. I was pretty much freaking out—a bit hooked on impression, still!

She and I had been getting to know each other by video and phone for over 3 weeks, and one September Saturday, over breakfast, we sat in awkward, awe-filled silence for the first few minutes and then picked up right where we left off. We ended up spending the entire day together touring the mundane and magical spots of Santa Monica Pier. We wandered through shops, caught ourselves checking each other out, and tried each other's food. We wandered for nearly 10 hours, stopping to talk, people watch and sometimes sit in silence with each other.

I was a king, walking beside a queen. She was stately and elegant. I was taking in all of our interactions and her treatment of those we encountered. When she watched the street performers and musicians she wondered about their stories... their journeys. I noticed an urge to fix my posture—to stand taller. In every conversation, at every turn, we fed each other intellectually, challenged ourselves emotionally and stretched each other spiritually. She freely offered her heart and risked vulnerability in ways I simply had not experienced before. I was emotionally available to receive this force of nature. As we talked, I realized that my Partner Vision had been exceeded and completely blown away by this woman.

As the sun began to set and my red-eye flight back to Chicago drew closer, we both sensed that we wanted to slow down time. Before we knew it, my time to leave had come. As we parted ways we hugged, and with a tear in her eye she kissed me softly and said, "Thank you." Her passionate embrace washed through me like warm, fragrant essential oil.

The next day, I looked at my dating accounts, filled with new matches and messages. I closed each one, then closed my laptop. I thought to myself, would I have been ready for her if I hadn't started this dating adventure? I can't say for certain, but I'm so glad I did. I don't think I would've been as equipped for such a deep connection and mutuality. I now knew how to accept and receive what she was giving to me. I'd healed. I felt like I was ready to love and be loved again. It was worth every single encounter. 3 months and over 100 dates later, I sensed that I was about to embark on a new relationship adventure. I was ready.

I took a walk through a balmy, beautiful Downtown Hyde Park with a massive smile and an overflowing heart.

I knew I'd be with her again soon.

I took a deep breath, and let it go.

THE END

For more resources on thriving relationships and to learn more about Coach KJ's online courses and in-person events, visit coachkj.one

About The Author

Kevin Anthony Johnson is an author, speaker & professional certified coach teaching local & global leaders how to build authentic, impactful relationships for over 20 years.

KJ is father to three young adults and enjoys spending time with them in the Woodlawn neighborhood of Chicago, Illinois.

Other Resources From The Author:

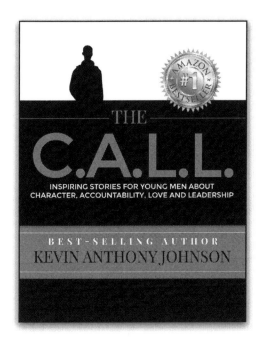

Available on Amazon.com

Made in the USA
Middletown, DE
03 December 2018